THE 'AND' PARADIGM

OWN YOUR EDGE, LIVE INTENTIONALLY, AND CAPTURE THE ULTIMATE PICTURE OF WEALTH

THE 'AND' PARADIGM

OWN YOUR EDGE, LIVE INTENTIONALLY, AND CAPTURE THE ULTIMATE PICTURE OF WEALTH

DUSTIN SERVISS

ethos
collective

Printed in the United States of America

Published by Igniting Souls
PO Box 43, Powell, OH 43065
IgnitingSouls.com

LCCN: 2025901790
Paperback ISBN: 978-1-63680-459-0
Hardback ISBN: 978-1-63680-460-6
eBook ISBN: 978-1-63680-461-3

Available in paperback, hardcover, and e-book.

To order copies of this book for your company,
please contact info@ServissWealth.com.
ServissWealth.com

First Edition
Print ISBN: 978-1-988602-03-5

I dedicate this book to my loving and patient wife, my two sons, my mother, my father, and all the mentors who have shown up at just the right time in my life.

Table Of Contents

My Story

May 15, 2016: Driving home feeling ashamed, disappointed, and somewhat scared that I was losing my mind.

I had organized for someone to babysit our six-month-old at the gym that day while my wife and I tried to put in a workout together—something we used to do side-by-side before our parenthood journey. Something that used to be our "thing."

For the past five years, while we dealt with many fertility complications and continued failed pregnancies, I had somehow managed to drown myself in my work. We had not worked out together, or connected for that matter, for a long time, and our marriage was in jeopardy. The solution was simple: work more and try not to think about it. The problem will solve itself, or it will go away.

From a very young age, my brain was wired to think a man could be "either" successful in his business "or" successful in his personal life, but not both.

It made perfect sense. If you focus on your business and earn more, you could provide more for your family and have more time or resources for your hobbies, ensuring a happier life.

But on May 15, I walked up and down our house, not knowing what to say to my wife or how to look my tiny baby in the eye. I had organized the babysitting at the gym for 4:30 p.m. and called my wife to let her know all was taken care of, and we would work together again. She was thrilled, explaining how she appreciated me taking the initiative to be more present.

Then 4:45 p.m. rolled around, and my wife called my office. "Aren't you coming to the gym?" she asked.

"I'll be right there."

And all I heard was "Don't bother" and the click of finality.

I sat at the kitchen table in tears with a huge lump in my throat. I didn't know what to do. Psychiatrist, psychologist, marriage counselor, life coach? What person can fix this? What person can fix *me*?

I cleared my schedule the following day in my office and figured out where the problem lay. I was successful, day-to-day money was taken care of, business was growing, and my health and body were in decent shape. *I can do this,* I thought.

Throughout the morning, I kept asking myself how I could be both financially successful and available to my family simultaneously. What does "available" actually mean? It isn't money. What about time? What about space in my brain so the gym situation would never happen again?

I took a deeper look at why I missed the gym session and noticed that in the past few years, I had not made time for any activities outside of work, whether for my family or myself. Instead, all my focus revolved around my job. But why? Out of fear—fear that the money would stop or that the business would fall apart.

I pulled out all our finances and laid them out on a massive spreadsheet. What would happen if I made a little less? If I saved a little less or hired another assistant, what would the financial picture look like at fifty-five years old, sixty, or sixty-five... guess what! It didn't look that bad.

If I saved a little less, I could spend more on family life upgrades like daycare two days a week. I could increase staffing at work and gain flexibility during the day to attend to child and wife matters. And I'd still be on track financially for retirement and the goals of the business.

The morning of May 16 was my turning point. The point at which my belief system started to change. The day I started replacing my "either/or" with an "and."

No more "either a successful business or a great family life" or "either a successful business or a life filled with personal hobbies." But instead, "Both a successful business AND the personal life I have always imagined."

You need more "ands" in your life.

Behind Grandma Mae's Microwave

My grandmother Mae dreamt of going on a cruise her whole life. She talked about it with my mother for years. After she passed away, we found an envelope wedged behind her microwave, stuffed full of brochures and rate sheets for luxury cruises worldwide. She had the money to go on those trips, but she died having never gone, with extra money in the bank. Why didn't she book the trip? What was she waiting for?

Does this sound familiar? It's a story I see again and again in my wealth management practice: Mid-career professionals strive to save for a secure future at the expense of their health, relationships, and mental well-being.

Why are *we* saving?

We say we're doing it for our family, fame, future opportunities, or old age security. But it boils down to this: most people continue to save to achieve more happiness or create the impression of ultimate happiness.

We think we'd be happier if we could do one more deal, open one more store and office, sign one more contract, hire one more employee, buy one more piece of real estate, or boost up our investment accounts. Or maybe we'd be happier if we did another course, worked one more weekend, or gave up one more hour of family time. We justify the sacrifices by telling ourselves that it will all pay off in the future.

But will it? Who says this is the right way to live? Our parents? Who told them? I don't know about you, but the belief in over-saving for the "future" doesn't seem to make sense anymore, especially when it happens at the expense of the "present."

For most of my adult life, I played along. I, too, believe that sacrifices now are supposed to lead to a better, happier, more fantastic life in the future. But I never really sat back and wondered how far out the future was or how hard I was supposed to work and for how long. I just knew to work hard and get somewhere in life.

We justify the sacrifices by telling ourselves that it will all pay off in the future.

Over many years, I had manufactured a story that we always had financial alligators swimming around us. We didn't, but you never know, I always thought. I was operating from a place of fear. Fear of losing everything paralyzed me until I started to internally challenge my thoughts.

This curiosity led me to make new connections and revisit old ones, starting fresh conversations with people I had met throughout my life—people who were financially comfortable and living beautiful lives but without all the stress and flash so many of us fall prey to.

The story you are about to read is patterned after those conversations. These people are not celebrities, social influencers, or billionaires. I guarantee you have never heard most of their names. But they have great relationships with their children, they have been married to the same spouse for decades, and their financial lives align with their lifestyles.

Some have stocks, others have real estate, some are entrepreneurs with small businesses, and some work jobs they love and have neither stocks nor real estate.

What can we learn from these people to ensure that when we look back on our lives, we can say: "I didn't miss a thing"?

What they all have in common is their mental shift towards The "And" Paradigm.

What is wealth? It's a bigger picture than you think.

This book can be your key to unlocking a new way of thinking about wealth, lifestyle, saving, spending, scarcity, and financial fear. We're told to work hard, be good, do the right thing, consider everyone's feelings, take the path of least resistance, not to spend, and, above all, *save, save, save.*

But if you do as you're told your whole life and always keep your powder dry, think about this: can you ramp up your retirement spending to live those phantom dreams without a massive conflict of beliefs? Or will you be like my grandmother who, even when she finally had the means and the time, still wouldn't spend the money to take herself on the trip of a lifetime? She was *still* saving for later. How will you suddenly change your thinking, your whole way of life, when you're too tired, too sick, or, let's face it, not even around anymore? That's why taking your foot off the brake *now*, while you have the resources and the agility, is so important.

Don't pass away with the ghosts of your dreams
behind the microwave.

The Question

"Hey, photo guy! How do *you* plan to retire?" The guys in the jeep, all with net worths cresting $100 million, all clutching craft beer cans and cigars, turned to hear Theo's reply with amused looks on their faces.

Theo blinked, thought momentarily, and realized he had no idea what to say. He'd been drilling these guys with questions about their businesses all weekend, and having the tables suddenly turned caught him off guard.

Theo recalled all his conversations in the last four years while trying to win the Ultimate Picture of Wealth contest. He thought about Omar, the Italian car parts zillionaire, Kaz, the unlikely farmer, and Carlos, the famous scuba diver in Cabo. They all had different things to say about how they achieved their wealth and what they valued. But Theo was literally in the middle of questioning his approach.

He also thought about Mans, the old caretaker of the luxury retreat where these men had each spent an average person's annual salary to enjoy four days of fishing and drinking expensive booze. How did he want to retire? With all these people and conversations in mind, the first thing that came to Theo's mind was "*happy.*"

"Happy," he said aloud, knowing before opening his mouth that these guys would laugh their heads off. "I want to retire *happy*."

From the front seat, Roy Duran, Canadian oil tycoon and Theo's current subject for the contest, guffawed loudly. "Yeah, but first, you must cash out with a significant financial win to live on. *That* is how you retire happy, my friend."

Theo tried not to inhale the cigar smoke and shifted in his seat. "Yeah, I guess." He was a little embarrassed to talk about his finances with people so far ahead of him in the game.

Their fishing guide, Orson, cut in: "Five minutes to the honey hole, boys."

The others returned to their beers and conversations as the jeep headed toward the far end of the lake. But Roy's question kept ringing in Theo's head. What *about* his retirement? At his graphic design and marketing firm, he'd built up an excellent library of stock photos and images, which provided a steady income.

"Hey Roy," Theo said. "You know what you said about cashing out? I get paid every time someone downloads one of my photos online. I'm set as long as that revenue covers my bare minimum expenses. I make money doing nothing! That's how I'm going to retire."

The three rich guys chuckled. Bill said, "My bare minimums are golf, boat gas, club fees, and good wine. The bigger the bills, the happier I must be!" They laughed.

"Do I have to include my ex-wife's jewelry shopping habit in my bare minimum?" Roy asked, and they laughed even louder. Theo thought about how many ex-wives these men must have between them, and then he thought about his wife, Ashley, who was at home that very moment, angry at him.

He was confused. These were wealthy men, successful men. He assumed they had made good investment decisions and probably worked hard to save the vast fortunes they had now. They got to do bucket list things, like this incredible trip. But he wasn't sure doing expensive things and bragging about them was considered wealth.

He thought about the fights he and Ashley had whenever he dug in his heels about something money-related and the sacrifices they'd made. His intentions were good; he thought if he made a decision that brought in more money, his family would be better off and happier. But it seemed like more and more of those decisions just made his wife angrier and angrier.

Orson pulled into a clearing near the shore, and the mist-covered cove appeared. Watching the others mill around putting on their fishing gear, Theo pondered why he was there: to capture the "Ultimate Picture of Wealth."

But he was starting to question whether being *wealthy* and being *rich* were revealed by similar pictures.

Ask yourself: Is the mission I am on worthy to me?

1

Think Fast, She's Hot

First Contest—12 August 2016
Austin, Texas

The energy was contagious as Theo entered the conference area of Austin's newest ultra-chic boutique hotel and micro-conference center. This was Theo's first attempt at capturing a winning photo for the Ultimate Picture of Wealth contest. He was meeting Omar Ansari in the one percenter's penthouse suite in an hour, but he wanted to take a moment to relax and "get his head in the game," as it were. His flight from Vancouver had been delayed, and he'd raced over straight from the airport. He was frazzled and more than a little nervous.

According to signs everywhere, the hotel hosted the sales awards for *Liv-Now!* Health Products, which looked like a line of women's nutrition and longevity beauty products. He approached the lobby bar and asked the bartender for a soda and lime. "What's all the cheering in the next room?"

The bartender smiled as she prepared his drink with a flourish. "Oh, this is the main event for all the top sales-women in North America. They come here every year. A rep must earn more than a million a year to qualify. They're great tippers."

Theo raised his eyebrows and took a seat at the bar. As he sipped his drink, he could not help but tap his foot on his bar stool. The pump-up music, laughter, and cheering from the conference room were infectious, and he wished he could join in. He turned around to people-watch from his barstool just as the conference room doors swung open. Some two hundred people, almost all women, poured into the surrounding halls and lobby. They were glowing, talking, laughing, and checking their phones. Theo noticed they wore name badges of different colours.

"What's with the badges, do you know?" Theo asked the bartender.

"The colours signify how many days off per year the person takes. How about that, huh?"

"No way."

"No joke." She turned and headed down the bar to serve another patron.

This was a twist Theo had never encountered. These people made great money and celebrated big goals, and they focused on days off. Theo looked at the nearest sign and typed "Liv-Now! Health" into his phone. It was a global company with an old-school multilevel marketing feel.

Through the crowd, Theo noticed one woman with a cluster of five or six others waiting to talk to her and take selfies. He asked for another drink, and when he turned back around, the group had dispersed and the queen bee was approaching the bar. She sat down two seats from Theo. She was hard not to look at. She practically sparkled with energy and smelled how Ashley smelled after she'd been at a spa: delicious.

Everything about her said money. Her clothes were expensive, and her black hair was styled into a perfect mass of curls. She wore dark, well-fitted jeans and a white T-shirt with a deep V-neck that contrasted attractively with her dark skin. It read *Excuse Me While I Succeed* in big, block letters. Artfully applied gold eyeshadow shimmered from her eyelids to her high, arched eyebrows, and expensive-looking rings adorned most of her fingers. The woman emanated confidence. Theo read her badge: Chloë Ellis. She ordered a Gin and Tonic.

In university, Theo was a full-scholastic volleyball player and captain of his team. He'd won sports and business awards after graduation and had attended many networking events where he was comfortable making small talk. He may have lacked financial confidence lately but always felt okay initiating conversations, especially with women. But this woman challenged his confidence; she nearly hummed with it herself.

She and the company intrigued him—specifically, how they created the infectious energy he had just witnessed. What made this group buzz? Theo faltered, feeling himself exiting his comfort zone. But he took the chance.

"Did you win an award today?" Theo asked. It was the first thing that came to mind.

She said, "Pardon?"

Shit. I should be focusing on my interview, not sitting at a bar chit-chatting. But he stuck to the game plan. Unable to fabricate a new entry point, he asked again, "Did you win an award today?"

"Oh," she said. "No, I was presenting this year."

"Oh, wow. That's great," Theo replied rather lamely. "I mean, the energy in that group is insane. If you ladies could bottle that, you'd be millionaires."

She smiled. "That's kind of what we do. And we *are* millionaires."

Oops. He knew that. A number of the women from the lobby had come to sit at the bar. Most were casually dressed—no power suits or cocktail dresses—and all seemed laid-back and friendly. Their laughter helped him relax.

He turned back to Chloë and said, "I'm Theo."

She shook his hand. "Chloë. You're here for the realtor convention?"

"No, I'm a photographer."

"Oh! Are you on an assignment?"

"Sort of. I'm trying to win a contest. The assignment is to take the 'Ultimate Picture of Wealth.' So, I'm here meeting my subject."

Chloë turned in her seat and looked Theo up and down, looking interested for the first time. He had the distinct feeling of being sized up. Chloë leaned in, looking him in the eye. "So, tell me, Theo, what does the 'Ultimate Picture of Wealth' look like?"

He was surprised at her directness—Chloë wasn't one for small talk. "Well, they want me to capture a wealthy person in their element, doing something only wealthy people can do. The photo I'm hoping for this year will be of an industry captain making a potentially billion-dollar deal." He stopped and looked around the bar, buzzing with Chloë's amped-up colleagues. "I have to be honest, I'm intrigued by your group. Many of you earn over a million, you said?"

"That's right," Chloë said. "And we're all independent operators. The thing that sets us apart, though, is that lifestyle is intentional for us. The mantra of the company is family, fun, *then* finances. We've all bought into being happy first, achieving success over time, and really trying to enjoy the journey along the way instead of sacrificing our lives to pile up a lot of money." She seemed to consider him for a moment and then leaned in. "I have a question for you, Mr. Wealth Photographer."

"Yeah, for sure." Theo was pleasantly surprised she'd chosen to keep the conversation going.

Chloë set her empty glass down and nodded at the bartender for another. She said, "If you're studying wealth, consider this. If I sell my company at age sixty and then die at sixty-three, I die with money in the bank regardless of whether I sold for $3 million or $1.5 million.. So, one could ask, should I have lived more of my life and sold for $1.5 million instead?

The thing that sets us apart is that lifestyle is intentional for us.

Theo thought about that for a moment as they sipped their drinks. His working life felt like building more, saving more, and trying to show everyone he was doing well. He finally just blurted out, "I don't know. How would *you* define wealth?"

Chloë paused, considering Theo, then moved to the stool beside him. She asked the bartender for some more napkins.

"I assume you're not doing origami," the bartender said, giving her a pen too.

Chloë pushed the pen and napkin over to Theo. "Show me what you think you know about this 'ultimate picture.' Draw what you think wealth looks like."

Theo stared at her. He was on the hot seat now. Well, he could start with having enough money to support your family and do what you want, when you want. He drew some boxes on the napkin and labelled them *expenses, assets, savings/loans,* and *investments.*

He showed her, but she slid it back to him. "Good start. Now flip it over and break it down. Be more specific."

Theo turned the napkin over and started again. This time, he drew bigger blocks, and inside the bottom block, he wrote *expenses, savings,* and *assets.* He wrote *business costs, profits,* and *investments* in the upper block.

Chloë nodded. "That's better. But what's missing?"

Theo stared at the napkin with its clumsy boxes. He added spaces for real estate and the kids' education.

She took the napkin, pushed it aside, and grabbed a new one.

"But that's all money, Theo. What about the *rest* of your life? The most important parts." She started drawing and placed her napkin on top of Theo's when she was done. "Here's what you need to consider *in addition to* your money plan: mental nourishment, physical health, and solid relationships with yourself and positive people. And my favourite: leisure spending. If you don't have a good lifestyle, you have *nothing.* Before a person can start investing in assets and savings, vehicles, or real estate, they need to see the value of investing in *themselves.*" She shoved the napkins back to Theo.

Theo looked over the napkins, which combined his original sketch with her ideas and expanded on them. He was floored to hear someone so successful talk about things like *friendships* and *self-care* as values above money. He'd always thought of those things as bonus items—side effects of being successful. He realized it had been a long time since he'd had a genuine emotional connection with a friend. His old friends had all faded as their careers started taking off.

Just then, four women entered the bar, laughing and excited. The smell of expensive perfume filled the air like a tropical breeze. One of them spotted Chloë. "Chloë, come on! A pop-up at a penthouse across the street—DJs and champers! Everyone's going!"

"Be right there," Chloë said, and with that, she threw a $50 bill on the bar and put her hand on Theo's shoulder. "I hope you capture that picture of wealth, Theo." She tapped his napkin diagram and winked. "Maybe you could enter an art contest if you don't win." And then she was gone.

Start enjoying what you desire for dinner and stop gazing down the right side of the menu.

2

Danger Zone Thinking

First Contest—31 May 2019
Vancouver, B.C.

"So, why couldn't Ashley and the kids make it tonight?" His mother's question snapped Theo out of his reverie. He was in his parents' kitchen, helping her make the usual Sunday dinner for him and his dad. They'd been jibing each other about fake news and politics as usual when he'd drifted away into his thoughts, chopping carrots with his mother talking away. Her abrupt question snapped him unpleasantly back to reality. She didn't need to say what she was thinking. Her tone said it loud and clear: *Why couldn't they make it tonight again?*

He'd been waiting for it.

"Kayla has soccer," he said lightly, but his mother's eyebrow rose slightly. He sighed. "And, truth be told, I'm in the doghouse."

He cleared his throat awkwardly and tried to sound confident. "I came home with a Harley a few weeks ago. She was over-the-top mad. I had shown her the ad before and even mentioned it was a good deal. She never objected. I thought that meant we had discussed it, but it didn't. She said she didn't think I was going to buy it." He didn't tell them what Ashley had said: *I didn't think you were that selfish.* Theo shrugged helplessly as his parents rolled their eyes. "I thought we were on the same page! We weren't. She says I need to communicate better, but I thought I had."

"Welcome to marriage, Theo." His mom replied. Theo bit his tongue and walked into the living room—time to change the subject.

Earlier that same week, he had gotten the call again, informing him he'd been handpicked to compete in the exclusive competition that had been dodging him for four years running. It was put on by *Ultimate Wealth International,* a glossy annual magazine with a small circulation that found its way into only the wealthiest hands. The prestigious competition attracted photographers from all over the world, yes, because it was a huge accomplishment, but mainly because every year, the four finalists were flown to exclusive locations on the magazine's dime to capture their subjects in the most luxurious habitats. Making the final round meant an all-expense paid "working" vacation.

For Theo, the win would mean a considerable badge of legitimacy and a potential jump in revenue. His company was already doing well, but the victory would take his business to a new level if he played his cards right. He'd been obsessed with it for four years and had made the finalist roster three times but had yet to crack the final code to win. Plus, he'd *promised* his wife he would give up after last year's loss. It was all-expenses paid, but he always spent a chunk of his own money anyway, which was a big bone of contention between him and Ashley. For this reason, he hadn't yet shared his "good" news with her and was dreading it.

Theo coughed nervously as his mother joined them in the living room and settled into her chair. "So, don't tell Ash because I haven't told her yet, but I entered the Picture of Wealth contest again this year." He casually leaned onto the coffee table to pick a cucumber spear off the tray, "And I heard this week I'm a finalist again." He tried to sound excited but couldn't quite pull it off. He knew exactly what was coming.

His dad put down his glass of wine.

Here we go, thought Theo.

"I don't mean to be negative, son, but isn't this little side project going to take you away from your actual work that pays actual bills?"

His mother nodded, narrowing her eyes at him while hooting with laughter. "And I thought you told Ashley you weren't entering again. You think she's mad *now?*" Theo bristled, feeling his face getting hot.

His dad continued, "Look, Theo, I know this seems exciting to you—flying somewhere flashy and hanging out with rich guys—but it seems like a waste of time. You're spreading yourself too thin to promote someone else's business. Seems like a scam if you ask me."

With an effort, Theo kept his temper in check and took a breath before responding. "Well, yes, of course, Dad, everything's got some marketing angle these days. I'm in marketing, remember? But I'm telling you, the contest is legit. I wouldn't be doing it if it weren't."

He resented his parents' patronizing tone. They'd been over this ground before. Whenever Theo tried something outside the status quo, his father had a particular way of knocking the wind out of his sails.

Theo tried to lighten the mood by laughing it off. *Maybe Dad is right!* he thought. He could feel his enthusiasm slowly turning into doubt.

"Well, anyway," his mother said, raising her glass to Theo and sipping. "I hope you win." The subtext of her statement was clear: *I hope it's worth it.*

• • •

Driving home from his parents' house, Theo's thoughts wandered. Ashley and Theo had been married for fourteen years and always had a great relationship until recently. They'd been sniping at each other and fighting more often than ever.

He opened the front door quietly, entered his house, and sheepishly approached the living room to find Ashley on the couch. The TV was on, and she was looking at her phone. She didn't even glance up.

"Sorry, I'm late."

She raised an eyebrow and continued scrolling. "Uh-huh."

"Ash," Theo finally said. "I have to tell you something. I entered the Picture of Wealth contest again this year and qualified. I said I wouldn't, but I just, well, I just did. Honestly, I didn't think I'd get in again. It just feels like they want me to try one last time. After this, I swear I will not enter again."

"When is it?"

"It's, uh, on Tuesday. We would leave on Tuesday."

She looked at him like he was crazy and then laughed. "You're kidding. That's hilarious. There's no way I could get the kids organized by then. And whatever happened to try

31

to communicate more? Maybe I could have gone too if you had told me sooner."

She turned back to her phone, shutting him out. "How nice for you. We'll be fine here without you. We're used to it. You do you. Hope you find what you're looking for."

He hated the hurt look on her face. And he hated being in this position: not being able to follow his passion without it seriously disrupting their lives. He resented not having unjudged access to extra funds and missed his spontaneous adventures with his wife.

But, more often than not, exciting adventures are not born from an endless series of logical thinking.

3

High Altitude Awakening

Fourth Contest—11 June 2019
9:30 a.m., A helicopter pad outside Pemberton

"You must be Theo!" The dreadlocked Aussie shook Theo's hand and took his bags. The sound of the waiting helicopter's propeller filled the air with anticipation.

He had just arrived at the helipad south of Pemberton, and the chopper was already waiting to take him to Permission Peak Lodge, where he would meet Roy Duran and his buddies.

"Have you ever been in a chopper before?" The guy handed Theo the clipboard and showed him where to sign. The sheet flapped under his hand from the wind. The chopper was kicking up.

"Yeah, lots of times," Theo couldn't help but take the opportunity to brag a little to this kid who was probably half his age. "I was a tree planter back in the day and a backcountry guide during college."

"Awesome, you know the drill then: always keep eye contact with the pilot when approaching or walking away from the machine."

"Ten-four."

Theo's heart started pumping as he hurried with the attendant to hop in. He was not only excited to be lifting into the air for a one-of-a-kind trip through one of the world's most beautiful mountain ranges but also anxious to meet Roy, an oil industry legend who, according to Theo's research, was happy and had business and life all figured out. He'd made some ballsy moves in the early 2000s and was now sitting on a pile of cash. He appeared to enjoy retirement on a large ranch east of Edmonton. Older pictures showed he had a beautiful young wife and several adult kids.

Theo couldn't wait to pick this guy's brain while he photographed him doing rich guy stuff in pristine nature.

His headset clicked, and the pilot turned to speak to him in a friendly, French-Canadian accent, a big moustache and a grinning smile showing from under his aviator shades and helmet.

"Hi, Theo! Welcome aboard, my man. My name is André. Let me know if you feel sick or will pass out, okay? I'll crack a window." He laughed at his joke. "We've got a twenty-two-minute ride, so get comfy." He clicked off and concentrated on lifting the chopper up and into the air, heading north.

Soon, Theo could see massive mountain peaks far in the distance and the sparkling Pacific Ocean to the horizon—one breathtaking view. To the right and just below as they passed, he spied a landing pad near the top of a jagged mountain, where another chopper was dropping off a group of mountain bikers. The pad was no more than 400 square feet of levelled dirt outlined with logs, with the mountain running down nearly a thousand feet on either side.

Watching the group from above, Theo felt a pang as he realized how long it'd been since he'd had anything he would call an adventure. The summer after graduating high school, he'd worked as a fishing guide, and then throughout college, he had guided a few snowcat and heli-ski trips during winters near Sicamous. But that was over ten years ago, and he hadn't been anywhere nearly so remote since.

"You from Alberta too, Theo?" The pilot's voice buzzed in his ear, interrupting his thoughts.

"No, just Vancouver." Feeling like that made him sound boring, Theo added, "Hard to beat all we have there."

"You one of those big movers and shakers going up for the fishing weekend?"

"Hardly."

"Dude, we got twenty minutes in here! Don't make me talk to myself."

Theo paused, then decided since he probably wouldn't see this guy again anyway, he might as well talk. "Well, I'm here for a contest. It seems like a dumb idea the more I talk about it. I'm supposed to capture the 'Ultimate Picture of Wealth.' Do you know what that is?" Theo laughed. "I've been trying to win this contest for the last three years, but I guess I'm not getting it. The irony is, I'm neglecting my own business while doing it." *And pissing off my wife,* he added to himself.

André didn't say anything, so Theo kept going. "I don't know, man. My dad worked for forty years at the same company to reach the top of the corporate ladder. He travelled

180 days a year, making deals and generating substantial revenue for his employers. He did okay, but we never saw the guy, and I know he wasn't that happy. And now, he's retired and has a nice house and freedom, but he's not *that happy*. You know? And now I see myself doing the same thing. A lot of my friends, too. Doing what their parents did, just working and saving, working and saving…" he trailed off, feeling a bit embarrassed.

"Well, money makes the world go round, right?" André said and laughed.

Theo looked out the window, thinking about the things he was most proud of when he was younger. He used to have a passion for exploring the road less travelled and flirting with risk. He loved discovery and didn't care what others thought. He wondered why that same guy was now trying to dazzle his neighbours with his lawn and his well-behaved kids, impress his in-laws with his luxury SUV, and inspire his employees with his nonstop work ethic.

André spoke up. "I work long hours, too. This is my chopper, and she takes a lot of maintenance. I have to run her around the clock to make good money. I get in shit at home sometimes for working too much, but I always think I'm doing it for them. My wife is great most of the time, but she tells me I'm doing it so I can buy a new Harley and go and play with my friends! Who knows what the answer is, Theo."

Theo laughed. "No shit. I'm going through the Harley thing right now, too! My wife is constantly telling me I put my job before everything, but when I buy something just for fun, she's pissed. I can't win!"

"Oh man, we could have a severe bro chat and figure it out for the rest of the world," André laughed.

He let Theo zone out for the rest of the ride as they floated over majestic ice-capped mountains and sparkling remote lakes.

As the sound of the chopper faded away, Theo found himself in a wide clearing, surrounded by the silent vastness of the mountains and a dense forest. The wind blew through the nearby trees, and an eagle called somewhere. It occurred to him that he had not read the instruction email from the lodge and felt a twinge of panicky anxiety setting in. He started to sweat, and his heart started beating faster. *What the hell, man? You used to* love *the unknown.*

He'd just taken out his phone even though he knew there was no service, when out of the trees about forty feet from the landing pad came a four-seater side-by-side utility vehicle, the driver honking the horn and waving. He pulled up alongside the stack of boxes André had left and nodded at Theo as he hopped onto the tarmac. "You must be the photographer. I'm Mans Jonsson. Get in—won't be a moment."

Mans was a big man, about seventy, Theo guessed, strong with a braid of thick, greying blonde hair down his back and a longish beard. He wore cargo pants and a company T-shirt with "Manager" embroidered on the chest, but even in that uniform, he looked more like a tough biker than anything else. He spoke with a subtle accent that Theo couldn't quite place. He wondered how this rough-looking man had found his way to this luxury lodge in the mountains.

Once they were seated and burning along the bumpy forest trail, trying awkwardly to reach out his arm behind the tight seats, Theo said, "Boy, you must think you've died and gone to heaven working up here. This is paradise!"

Mans looked over and winked inexplicably. "This trip will give you some views you've never seen, Theo. I can promise you that."

Just when the UTV emerged from the trees, Permission Peak Lodge came into view. It wasn't huge, but it was well-built and had been recently updated to a more modern design from the original structure, which Theo knew was many decades old. There were full-size windows on two sides of the main building, and Theo could see where a substantial wing had been added, almost doubling the footprint but maintaining the simple yet elegant look. The cabin—if you could call it that—backed onto a pristine lake surrounded by looming mountains. The water was clear and still.

Climbing out of the UTV, Theo could hear someone chopping wood somewhere, a sound he hadn't heard in ages. His heart tugged a little, remembering childhood camping trips. He looked around, trying to find the campfire he could smell, then noticed a chimney rising above the red steel roof, emitting a faint smoke trail into the sky.

"So, you live up here full time?" Theo said.

"Sure do."

When was the last time you ventured into uncharted territory?
Is it finally time to create a few new stories in your life?

4

Grab Another Gear

First Contest—12 August 2016
Austin, Texas

O mar Ansari was born and raised in Doha, Qatar, but emigrated to Italy as a young man. There, he spent the next fifty years building his empire, supplying the world's most expensive car manufacturers with the world's most expensive parts, systems, and technology.

Ansari Spec Industries made a name for itself in the seventies, designing specialty parts for supercars from Ferrari, Lamborghini, Alfa Romeo, and Maserati. Omar didn't stop there. Throughout the eighties and nineties, his hands-on management expanded the company into international manufacturing and industrial markets, all while maintaining its reputation for high-end, skilled production.

Omar's team had descended on Austin to meet with a major North American automaker that wanted its new hybrid super-vehicle technology. Theo would try to capture the CEO when he secured the potential nine-figure deal.

He thought if he shot the scene just right, he could somehow capture what had made Omar so successful. If he could do that, he would secure his win in the competition. Another part of him just wanted to talk to the man about cars. Theo had always been a Formula One™ fanatic as a kid. Safe to say, he was more than a little excited to meet a big-time industry insider.

His research told him Omar had been married to his third wife, a former fashion model, for thirty years. He lived a quiet but luxurious life in the Italian countryside, and he protected his privacy carefully. Omar had property worldwide and a museum-quality car collection that Theo had fantasized about visiting one day.

An assistant led him to the penthouse suite, where Omar waited in a vast, open-layout living area with a full bar and an entertainment system. Theo tried not to look *too* impressed. Omar was seated on a low, white, leather sofa that looked more expensive than Theo's car in front of a large plate glass window revealing an endless view of Austin and its horizon. His light, casual suit fit him perfectly. The whole scene oozed wealth and luxury.

Omar invited Theo to sit across from him in a ridiculously comfortable armchair and ordered two scotches. Once settled, Omar leaned back and crossed his legs casually, bringing to mind the few photos Theo had found online of a young Omar posing on racetracks with drivers in front of assembly lines that he'd designed himself.

"So, Mr. Hardisty," Omar started—he had an interesting accent, sounding to Theo like a blend of Italian and his

Qatari roots, and spoke English very well. "I hear you've come a long way to photograph my wealth?" His eyes had a teasing glint, and Theo felt slightly embarrassed.

"That's right, sir, yes. To capture 'ultimate wealth' in a photograph. Or, try to, anyway."

Omar rubbed his chin thoughtfully. "And what, if I may ask, do you think 'wealth' looks like?"

Despite himself, Theo laughed gently with a hint of a shoulder shrug. "Well, to be honest, Mr. Ansari, I'm not sure. But I think it might be captured tomorrow in your meeting. If wealth isn't the moment when a 100-million-dollar deal is made, I don't know what is."

Omar stared at Theo while nodding. "So, you think wealth is what happens in a board room, do you?"

Theo frowned. "I—it's got to be a part of it."

Omar chuckled and reached for his drink. "*What is wealth?* Everyone can see my wealth. I can do anything I want! I have many homes and my aircraft. I own the world's rarest cars. The '64 Ferrari alone is worth many millions. Is that wealth?"

Seeing Theo hesitate, Omar laughed again. "When I was a child in Qatar, my family was very wealthy and traditional. I was obsessed with car racing and watched all the Grand Prix and Formula One races on television. I dreamt of working with the Formula One cars. I couldn't imagine anything else. Of course, my parents didn't take that seriously, and when I announced at sixteen I was going to study engineering to be a race car designer, they forbade it.

"But when I was old enough, I went to Italy alone and put myself through university. I spent long hours at the track, just watching those cars. Driving them occasionally was exhilarating, but my passion was how it all worked. I could study them for hours—the way they moved, the way they sounded, and what made them perfect racing cars.

"I became good friends with so many drivers, who would tell me how driving a good race car would feel, how the mechanics would work, and which parts would fail. I put all that passion and obsessive knowledge into my first parts. The result was pure art—that's what they say anyway— Ansari parts quickly became known as the best.

"Those were the days I felt wealthiest. As they say, I was 'firing on all cylinders,' creating and immersing myself in the products and the industry I truly loved. It was my edge, my 'wealth edge,' I'd like to call it. All that obsession as a young man, my experience in school or the field, driving, creating parts with my own hands, gave me a marvellous edge when it came time to grow the business."

"Your edge? Please tell me more about that, Mr. Ansari."

Omar smiled. "My natural passion, experience, and time spent on the tracks came through in my products and the way I did business. That edge translated into investors who trusted me and believed in my vision. I was operating at the crux of my abilities. I could anticipate the needs of drivers before anyone else. I was always one step ahead. My expertise gave me unparalleled confidence as a leader in the industry. I was invested, *heart and soul*, putting me ahead of my competitors."

Everything Omar said struck a chord with Theo. Last week, he had come across a video from Dan Sullivan, co-founder of Strategic Coach®, introducing the idea of Unique Ability®. The idea of possessing capabilities, characteristics, and values entirely his own intrigued him. Did Theo really have a unique approach and purpose to his life he could tap into? Theo started thinking about his own company and his waning interest in it. Lately, he'd felt like the only thing driving him was more profit—financial gain only, nothing more.

What was *his* edge?

Omar seemed to read his mind. "I can see you're considering your situation. Maybe you haven't found your 'edge' yet?" He then stood up gracefully, signalling the end of the meeting. Theo stood up as well. "But there is one thing I can tell you about your wealth edge, Theo. It's not hard to recognize, but you must actively look for it."

Your Unique Ability is a superpower more capable than all investment and career choices.

5

Risk Reward

Fourth Contest—11 June 2019
1:00 p.m., Permission Peak Lodge

Theo stepped out onto the deck and inhaled deeply. The mountain air was so clean he could imagine it curing him as he breathed it in. He looked into the woods and towards the lake and felt his shoulders starting to relax. Closing his eyes while settling into an Adirondack chair, he thought, *This is heaven.*

For the first time in a long while, he felt genuinely present. The fresh air and the serenity of the surroundings took his mind off work and personal problems, and the lack of wifi at the cabin meant he couldn't check in on anything even if he wanted to. He couldn't remember a single time in his life when he'd heard such silence. Even the birds seemed to be holding their breath when it was broken by footsteps below him and a friendly voice.

"I see you found the best seat in the house."

Theo turned to see a guy walking up from around the side of the cabin. He was about six feet tall, around Theo's age, wearing a retro M*A*S*H T-shirt and tapered khakis tucked into his tan military-grade boots.

"I'm Orson, your cook, waiter, guide, and first aid attendant." He walked up the stairs to the deck and reached out his hand. His handshake could crush beer cans. Theo noticed a pair of six-inch scars on Orson's forearm and a three-inch scar above his eyebrow. It seemed like Orson had found himself in some "situations" in the past.

"Theo."

Orson noticed Theo's high-end camera. "You're the photographer?"

"That would be me, here to capture the 'Ultimate Picture of Wealth.'" Theo made air quotes with his hands.

"For a contest, right?"

"Yes."

"Maybe you have a better idea of what wealth would look like. But I can tell you, after many years up here, I don't. I know what rich looks like."

"Well, I'm sure you know more than me."

"Oh? Why do you say that?"

"Well, I—I don't know," Theo stammered. Orson just looked at him expectantly, so he took a breath and kept talking. "I mean, I've always been driven to make more and more money. I was taught to save, save, save, right? Money kept me out of trouble and provided a focus when I would lose my way.

"Then, when I got a little older and had a family... well, lately, I've started to feel like my focus on money has become more of a distraction than anything else. Maybe it's just a habit. Sometimes, it's like I'm living for a future that will never come. And it's feeling more and more like this imaginary future is a lot more fun than the real present."

Orson nodded thoughtfully and crossed his big arms. "That makes me think of when I was a marathoner years ago. I was constantly in my head, thinking three races ahead, ignoring everyone around me. I lost some friends that way and a few girlfriends who didn't want to be 'race widows.' *One more win, shave one more minute*—that's all I cared about. Then, posting race results online became part of it. I was hooked on the approval I got from winning. When I stopped competing, that social engagement evaporated, and I had abandoned my real friends, too. It took me a while to rebuild a few key relationships. Do you think the same could be said for people so focused on money for the approval of others?"

Just then, Mans came up the deck stairs. "You boys getting philosophical already?"

Orson laughed and saluted Mans. "That's my cue! I'd love to stay and keep solving the world's problems, Theo, but I'm heading in to prep for dinner." He gave a peace sign and went into the lodge.

"Any questions so far?" Mans asked.

Theo shook his head. "No, but do you ever hear guests say they feel a sense of lightness coming here?"

Mans chuckled. "If they're lucky."

Theo pointed across the lake. "Does that peak have a name?"

"That, my friend, is Permission Peak. Do you want to get a better view?

"One hundred percent."

● ● ●

The UTV climbed a slope away from the lodge and came out on a bluff where, as promised, they got a comprehensive view of the lake. The water was crystal clear and still. The mountain's reflection on the opposite side was like a mirror image. Mans brought the machine to a halt and turned off the engine. Theo took his camera out and took a few pictures of the classic vista, playing with the mirror images. Time seemed to have stopped.

Mans nodded and said, "Many of our guests never come up to see the lake from here, even though we encourage them and provide a map. They're here to fish and only fish. They always want to know the biggest fish caught here or the most caught in one day. It is actually ironic, by focusing on the biggest fish, they completely miss the bigger picture."

Pointing to a spot in the middle of the lake, Mans said, "Do you see where the water is slightly darker?"

Theo shielded his eyes and squinted down at the lake. Sure enough, a dark blob was under the surface near the middle. He nodded.

By focusing on the biggest fish, they completely miss the bigger picture.

"That's a tight school of fish," Mans said. "They follow the stoneflies and sowbugs as those nutrients move around the lake with the wind. Now look over there." Before Theo could open his mouth and start talking about his days as a fishing guide, Mans pointed to an area near the far shore, where the bottom of an avalanche chute met an incoming stream, creating a pool slightly higher than the central part of the lake. A small shadow moved in the water there, too.

"Over there are the biggest, best-fed fish in the lake. The two areas don't always connect because there's a rock spine from the avalanche debris that separates that pool. The fish can only get there by finding their way over or around the spine. Because of the stream, the oxygen and nutrients are richer."

Before returning to the UTV, Theo aimed his camera at the hidden pool and took a picture. He didn't know why, but he wanted to remember those risk-taking fish.

People are programmed to follow the herd, but to have a world of abundance, we must embrace the possibilities of the unknown outcome.

6

Is Enough Worth It

Fourth Contest—12 June 2019
Early morning, Permission Peak Lodge

Theo emerged from his room to the pleasantly pungent aroma of freshly brewed coffee. Following his nose, he entered the kitchen and found Mans at an expensive-looking gas stove, boiling coffee in an old-style percolator. He was again wearing cargo pants and a company shirt, which appeared to be his uniform. His beard was trimmed, and his long white hair was combed and tied back neatly. He was a perfect picture of self-assured wellness. Life at the lodge agreed with him. Theo wondered what his story was.

"Coffee?" The caretaker asked as he set a steaming ceramic mug before Theo. Then, he poured himself one. It was a cozy, comforting scene with real cream and honey for the coffee, a pot of oatmeal bubbling on the stove, and a fresh morning breeze drifting through the wide-open windows.

Theo sipped his coffee briefly before asking, "What brought you up here anyway, Mans?"

Mans smiled and stroked his beard, apparently an old habit. "Well, that's a bit of a story, Theo. I came to Canada from Iceland in the seventies as a young, ambitious man. I was obsessed with the promise and industry of this country. I started a paving and gravel company and hit the ground running. I did well. It wasn't a national company, but I expanded until I was the main provider of stone and gravel for the whole province."

Theo stopped him. "Wait a minute. Jonsson Aggregate? That was your company?" He could remember seeing trucks on the road when he was a kid—lots of them.

Mans smiled. "I had locations in Vancouver, Kamloops, and Prince George. I made a lot of money and just kept going. I had a family and a nice house. I did all the things I was supposed to do. But after twenty years in the business, I realized I was miserable. I worked long hours, missing out on my kid's life, and I barely knew my wife. Also, I was sick. I'd already had two ulcers."

Theo set down his coffee cup, thinking about his recent heart palpitations and the anxiety he'd been meaning to talk to his doctor about. "This sounds familiar," he said.

Mans continued. "Everything started to sink in when I watched a close friend of mine die before fifty, then a business associate. I got scared and started questioning what we were all working so hard for and if maybe there was another way to live. That's when I stumbled across this place. A client was talking about selling his family's hunting cabin, and on a whim, I bought it. I needed a change and remembered how much I loved nature as a kid in Iceland."

"Wait, you *own* this place?" Theo slapped his forehead.

"Look, I know I don't look the part, but is it that bad?" Mans laughed. "Listen, Theo. You would not believe the conversations I have with people up here at the lodge. Really successful people at the top of their game seem to be completely missing the point of their lives."

Mans lowered his voice as the other guests trickled into the living area, looking for breakfast. Orson was now boisterously holding court at the table, serving coffee and bringing out pastries.

I got scared and started questioning what we were all working so hard for and if maybe there was another way to live.

"Between you and me, Theo," Mans leaned in confidentially, "sometimes I feel like telling these people that *being busy* is not a status symbol anymore. We've evolved since the eighties. Tell me how you've figured out to be there for your family and still run a successful business—*that* is status."

"Oh boy," Theo said. "Busted. I'm spending a week off in the mountains by myself, chasing a status win, while my wife and kids are at home. After this, I won't be able to take time off again for the rest of the year." He suddenly felt guilty.

Mans stood up. "Why don't you ask your wife to come up? If she could be at the chopper port by four tomorrow, she could catch the last flight of the day coming up with supplies and spend your last night here with you."

Theo hesitated. "Oh, thanks, Mans, but we really can't afford to."

Mans cut him off. "Don't worry about it. The chopper's coming anyway, and your rooms are already paid for. I'm sure your wife isn't a big enough eater to put us that far back in groceries," he chuckled and slapped Theo's shoulder. "Come into the office and use the SAT phone."

Theo relented, nervously followed Mans into the office, and picked up the phone. Five minutes later, after a tense conversation with Ashley, he hung up, feeling excited and nervous.

He'd convinced her, somehow, to leave the kids with his parents and come up. It meant a missed soccer practice and a piano lesson (that had already been paid for, Ashley was sure to point out), but something in his voice must have told her to put her pride and the kids aside to focus on the two of them, just for one day. Sometimes, he felt she would enjoy life more if she lowered her expectations just a little.

• • •

A few hours later, when Roy and his friends arrived, Theo was on the deck with a beer and his notebook. Even from the outside, he could hear the loud voices that seemed to be jockeying to be heard.

He quickly identified Roy as the group leader. He was a heavy-set man in his mid-sixties, very pale, with thinning, curly red hair oiled and brushed back from his forehead. Theo reached out and shook Roy's hand, noting the briskness of the exchange.

"How was the trip up?" Theo asked.

"Well, it would have been nice to have a cocktail in the chopper and a hot flight attendant to serve it," Roy guffawed. "But all in all, we're here, and we're looking to catch some big-ass high-mountain trout, aren't we boys?" The others cheered in agreement, laughing and slapping each other's backs. The smell of booze hovered around them like a haze. They must have been drinking on the car ride up from the Vancouver airport.

"Well, you sure have a great chance of snagging some excellent fish out here," Theo said awkwardly. "I've heard there's some great fishing in Alberta, though."

"I'm going to change my clothes," Roy announced, ignoring Theo's comment.

While the men checked into their rooms and got themselves situated, Theo took the time to make sure his gear was fully charged and in working order. He caught up with Roy's two mates, Bill and John, out on the deck, where they were enjoying the lake view for the first time, each already with a cigar and beer in hand.

"Roy's excited to have you along to take some pictures," Bill said. "This is for a contest or something, right?

"For sure," Theo said.

Bill wore a Ducks Unlimited® ball cap that looked like the tag had just been cut off. He had chrome-framed glasses and a scruff on his chin. It was clear he didn't get outside much. He looked about seventy, but Theo was sure he was younger than that.

Orson had now come out to the deck to meet the group and announce that dinner would be served shortly. Theo was struck by the difference between this man at the prime of his health and thriving and these older men of "industry" seemingly prioritizing different intentions. His earlier conversation with Mans drifted through his mind. *Sometimes, I feel like telling these people that being busy is not a status symbol anymore.*

Dinner consisted of sublime Kobe steak, fire-roasted vegetables, and several other courses. Orson's service to these men was impeccable. Everything was elegant and perfectly executed. Theo was starting to realize the high price tag of a holiday here.

After dinner, the scotch started to flow. As the evening went on, the stories got taller and more majestic but then shifted to how miserable the three new guests were in their marriages.

Roy had just divorced the pretty wife Theo had read about in the articles. She had been his second wife, and now he was a bachelor again at age sixty-five. He didn't seem happy about it. From what Theo could gather, he was spending a fortune on lawyer's fees. Theo tried to contribute to the conversation but couldn't relate—he didn't feel he was on the same level. "I need to get rested up," he said, saluting as he got up and took his leave.

"I could use some rest, too," Bill said. "But I sure needed this trip. I haven't taken a single day off in eight months!"

"Oh?" Theo said, turning back, as this had piqued his interest. "What's got you so busy?"

"One last push before I retire," Bill said. "I'm aiming for ten more stores before I sell out. That's in five years." He raised his glass, and the others toasted him.

"Really? *Why?*"

Bill looked defensive, reminding Theo of his dad several weeks earlier. "Ten more stores in five years. That will make forty in total. Seems like enough to retire on—my accountants think so anyway." he laughed, and the others joined him.

Theo, considerably more sober than the others but still with a couple of scotches under his belt, couldn't stop himself from raising his voice, "But don't you think you have enough *now?*" For some reason, Theo was feeling reckless and stood his ground. His head was full of all the thoughts he'd been having since he arrived at the lodge, and when else would he be able to grill someone like Bill about wealth?

There was an awkward silence, and then John said, "Bill has over a thousand employees and a team of full-time accountants right outside his office. He has people to do his thinking for him."

Theo got the hint. "You have a point there, John. Sorry, Bill. What do I know anyway? I'm just a photographer." He laughed, and the others did as well—luckily, all the booze and good food had them in fine spirits.

As he put his key in the door to his room, he noticed Orson coming down the hallway. "What about this lodge makes you love it so much?"

But don't you think you have enough now?

Orson propped the tray on his side and thought for a moment. "Well, if I have to think about it, I guess it's because it's always changing. I learn so much here, from the evolving landscape throughout the seasons to the people who come to stay from different parts of the world. I learn about myself and my life. That, and the thrill of exploration and the odd wolf or cougar encounter make this the perfect place for me. Living close to my values..." Orson paused, searching for the correct description, " It's *vibrant* here. I never feel static. And I get to be outdoors, being active all the time. At this moment, I realize my 'enough' came sooner than I told myself it would when I was younger, and it feels good.

"Now get some sleep. Big day tomorrow!" He clapped Theo on the shoulder as he walked towards the kitchen.

As he brushed his teeth, Theo considered what Orson said about being in the right place for his values. He couldn't help but envy the man a little. He wasn't sure he'd *ever* felt that way, not consciously. He tried to put it out of his mind and went to bed. Ashley would be joining him tomorrow.

If no one was watching or caring about your increased success, would you keep grinding for a little longer?

7

Magic Apology

Fourth Contest—13 June 2019
Permission Peak Lodge

Theo took hundreds of photos of Roy and his friends— shots of them holding up their catches before releasing them, pictures of them reeling a bent-over fly rod near a stream entering the lake on the far side, photos of them in their belly boats having a beer together in the middle of the lake.

Theo and his cameras accompanied Orson as he advised them and served snacks and drinks on the water. They also respectfully gave them lots of space to bond, and Theo tried to stay out of the way as much as possible, even hiking around and taking shots from the shore. He was proud of his work and felt confident the photos would beautifully document three friends relaxing together and letting their guards down: three tycoons in a rare, vulnerable moment.

He felt he was close. But had he captured the "Ultimate Picture of Wealth"? He didn't know. During the journey back to the lodge, the guys argued over who'd caught the biggest fish, and the usual comparisons of longer versus fatter were made along with the inevitable manliness jokes. Theo snapped a few candid shots of the guys arguing and laughing.

The banter continued as they entered the lodge where Mans had laid out appetizers: decadent charcuterie boards that looked like they could be in a food magazine and heaping baskets of crusty freshly made bread and artisanal crackers.

Theo's stomach started growling as he walked by the table. He thought of grabbing a quick sample bite, but he'd heard the chopper had arrived a while before their return and was excited to see his wife. Maybe by sharing this experience, he could return to her good books again.

When he entered his room, he saw Ashley's bag on the bed, torn apart with clothes trailing out of it in a tumble. He smiled, suddenly remembering that this was something he had first loved about her: the messiness that other people thought chaotic. He thought it was a charming sign of a free spirit. It had been long since he'd seen that side of her. When they became parents, she'd "cleaned up her act." But it looked like she'd decided to relax her own rules. Maybe the lodge already had the same effect on her as it had on him.

He leaned his head out the door and saw one of the shared bathroom doors was closed. He could hear the shower running. He returned to the room and sat on the bed, waiting anxiously.

It didn't take long for her to enter the room, towelling her hair and dressed in a robe. They exchanged nothing but awkward silence for a few moments, not knowing what to say. Finally, Theo stood up, went over, kissed her, and hugged her. She felt warm and smelled fresh. He had missed this familiar feeling and wanted to savour the moment.

"I'm sorry I haven't been around enough for you and the girls," Theo said into her ear. "I'm working on that. This place is making me see things differently. I want to try harder, okay?"

She hugged him back tightly. "I'm sorry, too. I've been a bitch. I should try to see your side, too, I know. I miss you."

Theo felt a wave of relief and love for his wife. Maybe they would be alright after all.

"How was the chopper ride?" Theo asked, starting to get changed out of his sweaty clothes. He was excited and proud to bring Ashley out to meet the guys. She was a great-looking woman, healthy and always smiling. She was also brilliant and had a knack for loosening up people in suits.

"Oh my God, I was a little nervous! But that pilot, André? He was awesome, explaining things and chatting with me. But it was cool!" Ashley said. "How did your shoot go today?"

"Good, I think. I got some solid shots. This place is magic."

"I know! I felt so relaxed as soon as I got off the helicopter. It's so quiet up here. I can't believe it."

Just then, there was a knock on the door, and Mans' voice came through the door. "Cocktail hour, folks!"

Your trajectory to wealth will instantly change with a heartfelt "sorry," even though you may not think you have to say it.

8

Diving Fearlessly

Third Contest—17 June 2018
Somewhere north of Cabo San Lucas

S ome years ago, Theo had come across a boutique dive shop in a small resort in Cabo San Lucas that catered to the ultra-rich. The owner seemed pretty interesting himself—he was a pioneer in the world of scuba diving. When Theo did a bit of digging out of curiosity, he learned that the fifty-two-year-old Carlos Reyes had participated in some of the most iconic and essential dive projects in the world, including capping rogue oil wells and managing dive operations for tidal energy projects. Most recently, he'd managed a team of forty divers constructing the world's deepest pillar bridge in South America. Theo was fascinated and wondered if Carlos was like the cowboy the bloggers and podcasters described.

Theo took a long shot for his third attempt at winning the contest: he called Carlos and struck gold. The diver said he had the perfect opportunity for him. He was about to guide a group of lawyers—partners in a multinational firm based in London—who all had personal incomes well north of several million a year. They dove with Carlos yearly, so Carlos knew they enjoyed living large and splashing their money around.

The resort required an early morning flight and a forty-five-minute bus ride. The bus was more like a shiny black shuttle van carrying them down a short, dusty dirt road and emerging onto a small but impeccable beach resort. The landscaping around the buildings was lush with gardens and a waterfall. Through the open-air lobby, Theo could see a sparkling pool. Another waterfall splashed into the pool, making it even more inviting. He had an hour to kill before starting scuba testing, so he quickly checked in and headed for the pool.

He had just settled in a deck chair with an iced coffee when he heard a booming voice call, "Theo, my man!" He looked up, and there was Carlos, striding confidently off the beach with wet hair and a towel around his shoulders. He had clearly just finished his midday beach routine. He was healthy, with a dark perma-tan and a stocky physique fed with fruits, vegetables, and plenty of exercise. Theo knew from an online article that Carlos dabbled with lifting and was an early adopter of ice baths.

"Wait!" Theo said on impulse, holding his hand out to halt the amused Carlos in his tracks. He picked up his camera and snapped a quick picture of the diver.

Carlos's passion for diving came out in every sentence. He exuded a sense of self-assuredness that put Theo at ease instantly. He had indeed found his calling working with these people. "I know you'll get the shot you need here," he told Theo. "These guys have everything."

"I appreciate you making this a reality for me, Carlos."

"Hey, I made it work with that magazine footing your bills," he winked. "Make yourself at home and enjoy the resort."

The lawyers arrived at the resort after sundown. Theo was relaxing on the pool deck when he heard the commotion of loud conversations and laughter. He turned in his lounge chair and saw about a dozen men—wearing expensive polo shirts and chino shorts, and a few were sporting brand-new fedoras.

• • •

Theo snapped photos of the lawyers for the next couple of days as they made their way around the resort. He captured everything from champagne toasts to enjoying small-batch craft beer that they had made Carlos import from Belgium. But it was now the second to last day, and Theo still hadn't found anything that qualified as contest-winning.

After breakfast, Theo walked around feeling his funk when he stumbled upon Carlos in the boat shed, organizing gear. "Hey, Theo," Carlos said. "Could you help me move this old fish tank? My maintenance guy is off and I need to get this out of here."

"Sure."

The two men carefully hoisted the tank and stepped away from the bench it had been resting on. As they shuffled outside with the tank between them, Carlos asked how the photo shoot was going, and Theo told him that the 'ultimate picture' of wealth was eluding him. "I don't think I even know what wealth is, you know? My business is good. I live the dream because I have a nice house and two nice cars. But I don't feel *wealthy*. I look at these guys, and they're just so *certain*. How do they even know that it won't all go to hell in an instant?"

Carlos nodded as they went back inside. On the wall, behind where the tank had been, was an old whiteboard with a faded diagram drawn on it. Carlos looked at the diagram and thought momentarily, his brow wrinkling as he turned something over in his mind. He scratched his head thoughtfully, his tattooed forearm rippling under the rolled-up sleeve of his universal white linen shirt. "Maybe you should imagine wealth or the journey to wealth as a scuba trip."

"Ahh, what?"

"What you said about everything going to hell in an instant. It made me think." Carlos pointed at the whiteboard where someone had drawn a triangle cut into sections. He explained how they used the pyramid as a pre-dive template to sketch out all the possible risks and variables. "We account for the weather, any hazards in the area, tides, anyone possibly sick in the group, or any long-latent claustrophobia—all the things that could pose any possible risk. We discuss how we will handle each one if it becomes an issue.

"I've seen so many people get fixated during dives on really low-probability events, like getting eaten by a shark. They're so focussed on the wrong risks they unknowingly expose themselves to the more likely risks, like coming up too fast or getting lost."

Theo took out his phone and snapped a picture of the pyramid. Then he turned to Carlos.

"Is that how you made all this happen?" He gestured around at the resort.

Carlos put his hands on his hips and grinned. "Well, I guess I did. I knew all the risks. I did tons of research and accounted for everything as much as possible; that way, I could focus on the adventure of it all instead of worrying about worst-case scenarios."

That day, Theo took almost 600 photos of the lawyers' final outing, capturing the journey going down the anchor chain, swimming among stunning tropical fish and giant rays, or being served food and drinks at the prow. This has to be wealth, Theo thought. *Being at the expensive resort surrounded by other rich people, not thinking about work as the law firm cranks out profit half a world away.*

Minor issues would pop up occasionally, but no one would notice. The staff dealt with everything efficiently and maximized the minutes on the trip. Just like he and Carlos had discussed earlier, everything was accounted for.

As the other men picked at a surprisingly comprehensive seafood buffet and got drunker, Theo noticed a pod of dolphins racing alongside the back of the boat, occasionally spiralling into the air. It was magical. He looked back to see if the lawyers were noticing, but they didn't look up from their talk.

He overheard Madog asking Carlos, "What's the biggest shark you've ever seen?"

With life priorities clarified, the daredevil of your identity can rise from the ashes.

9

Chaotic Automation

Fourth Contest—14 June 2019
Last day at Permission Peak Lodge

Theo got up early, showered, and headed out, letting Ashley have a well-overdue sleep-in. He grabbed his notebook, which had been lying unused at the bottom of his duffel bag. There was a steaming pot of coffee in the kitchen. Theo got himself a mug and headed to the living room to write down all the thoughts bugging him since he'd gotten there—all the things he'd talked about with Mans, Orson, Roy, and his friends, and André. He kept on writing. He wrote about Chloë, Carlos, Omar, and even his parents.

Mans joined in. "So, Theo, did Roy and his buddies give you your ultimate picture of wealth?"

Theo thought he heard the slightest hint of teasing in his voice. He closed his book. "Well, I took about a thousand photos yesterday, so I sure hope so." He paused, "But I must admit, the experience has challenged my intentions and ego. These guys are super rich. But they don't seem happy. They're still working with the same goal that they probably started with. Just—more." Theo gazed out the window.

Mans replied while sipping on his coffee. "What is the one thing you would think about a lot?"

"Easy money. And trying not to piss Ashley off."

"Let's get the easy part out of the way first: Money."

Theo laughed.

"Transforming from a money mindset to a wealth mindset does not have a finish line. Part of being truly present is embracing the chaos of not knowing everything all the time and letting it be okay. What worked for me, Theo, was reducing the brain time required to think about money by automating my mindset."

Theo leaned forward. He wished he could take notes without seeming like a total sophomore.

Mans continued. "Automating your money mindset comes when you have a goal to focus on. You move money regularly to productive places and then spend the excess cash. By freeing up your brain, you let new experiences into your field. Once you have that plan on autopilot, you can stop feeling guilty about allocating money to new conveniences like dry cleaners, lawn care, automatic car washes, bottle depot drop-offs, etc.

Part of being truly present is embracing the chaos of not knowing everything all the time and letting it be okay.

"With that new extra time, you can pursue what lights a fire in your belly. Yes, you may have a little less in your bank account, but you have a plan instead, which means you have protection. Now that you know you're saving enough, what are you saving more for?"

"I get that," Theo said. "But how do I know what to do if my goals don't seem to mean as much anymore or I feel off track?"

Mans shook his head. "Likely, you *must* let go of the goal being a *number*, Theo. Think of it this way." He grabbed Theo's notebook and opened it to a blank page, then drew an arrow with a wide squiggle going through it. "Imagine a water skier being towed behind a boat, doing a slalom course. That's you. You start straight, then come to the course and weave back and forth. That's navigating, experimenting, trying different things, and enjoying your life. It's okay because you're still going in the same direction as the boat toward your goals.

"The boat is your values, pulling you along. See? Yet the skier is pinballing side to side on the rope. But as long as you are crossing the wake and going back and forth but are still up on your skis, you are going toward the boat. As you pick up more knowledge and skill, you can shorten the rope, which means you're better and get faster on the course. Life is like that. If you look at a snapshot of the skier at a given instant, it may look like they're way off course, but if they're holding onto the rope—your vision—and getting faster each pass, they are very much on track."

"What happens if the skier falls?" Theo asked.

Before Mans could answer, Ashley came into the living room. It had been a while since Theo had seen how beautiful his wife was. He couldn't look away.

• • •

They took their coffee out to the lake and started a fire as they watched the morning sun creep along the length of the lake. They held hands and cuddled under a blanket, enjoying each other's company without the girls and work demanding their constant attention. Ashley was hilarious when she was ultimately off guard, and he hated that it had been so long since she'd been this relaxed around him, at least since their last holiday, over two years ago.

They were getting hungry when a tall woman appeared with a tray of pastries and a carafe of fresh coffee. It was Helena, Mans' wife, who had come down from the lodge to introduce herself. She'd been in Edmonton on a family visit and had come in early that morning. After the initial hellos, she turned to Theo. "Mans asked me to tell you that he's going to check on the water catchment system now, if you want to take a look. He said you mentioned you'd like to see it. I'll keep Ashley company while you're gone." The women laughed as Theo drained his coffee and hustled off.

"How did you sleep?" Helena asked as she took Theo's chair. She looked fresh, rested, and relaxed, dressed in functional khaki pants, a crisp blue Permission Peak polo shirt, and her light brown hair in a neat ponytail.

Ashley sighed contentedly and sat up. "Great. Thank you so much for having me up here, Helena. It's such a needed treat. Honestly, that was the best sleep I've had in a long time. I forgot what it feels like to be rested. And no kids to care for! It feels heavenly," she laughed.

"I know what you mean," Helena said. "This place changed our lives, Mans and me. We were so stressed before. Mans was driving himself to an early grave with that damned company. I was quite high up at a mining company based in Prince George. We were both just on the edge all the time. We barely saw each other. But coming up here changed everything. It sounds so cliché, but I don't know... slowing down lets us discover who we are. Our true curiosities started showing up, you know?"

Ashley nodded. "I can feel that," she said. "And I know Theo does, too. Usually, he's stressed and rushing around on a shoot, but I've never seen him so relaxed and at peace, almost like he doesn't care about it. He's been obsessed with this contest for years now, like he thinks if he wins it, it'll mean he's legitimated or something. I don't know what you've been feeding him up here, but it's working! I finally see what happiness looks like on him, you know?"

Helena smiled. "Yes, I do. We had that experience when we came up here, too. It's such a haven."

"How do you do it?" Ashley couldn't help but ask. "I mean, it's so remote, and working with your spouse is hard sometimes. I don't know if Theo and I would last up here without killing each other."

Slowing down lets us discover who we are.

Just then, Mans and Theo came out of the lodge toward the fire, Mans with two empty cups in his hand. It was still early, but Roy and his friends had already headed out with Orson.

"I still would like you to finish answering my question!" Ashley said after they'd all settled again.

To Mans' inquiring look, Helena laughed. "I've been imparting all sorts of wisdom about what this place has taught us about marriage. Care to consider how we try to make all this work?"

Mans smiled but didn't laugh. He put down the coffee cups and thought for a minute while the others looked on, amused. Finally, he spoke.

"I take that question so seriously, Ashley. What has this place taught us? I can't speak for my wife, but I know what it's taught *me*. I was married before to my high school sweetheart, who gave up everything in Iceland to move with me here when I decided on a whim I wanted to be a frontiersman in the Canadian wilderness. She was a teacher in Húsavík and loved her life there. But she dropped her job and followed me to live in Prince George of all places. She hated it there but never said anything, centring her life around supporting me and my business. I didn't find out how unhappy she was until after she died of cancer. I hated myself for a long time for not seeing it, for being so caught up in my pursuit of wealth and success. It took me years to forgive myself and her, as well, for never being honest about how she felt."

"And then I met this wonderful woman here." He reached out and took Helena's hand. "We do everything differently. We have our own lives and goals, but we live in tandem and support each other. Going from Manager to Owner was a decision we made together, with complete buy-in from both of us, and there is always the caveat that anytime either of us wants to do something different, that will be a conversation and a decision made together." He looked over at Helena, and she nodded approvingly.

"I would say, for me, the main thing I've learned since coming up here is never to let your agenda take away from your spouse and their goals. Helena thought long and hard about coming up here with me. It was a conscious decision that Anna never made. Helena still does stuff on her own and maintains her own life, which I respect, and she does the same for me. We make space for each other's autonomy, which also means financially. And remember, having your own goals is not selfish. It is crucial to the survival of important relationships."

Ashley thought about Theo and the contest and how she'd punished him for wanting to pursue his interest.

Theo thought about how he inadvertently controlled their money, leaving Ashley in the dark about where they stood financially.

They looked at each other. "We could work on that a little," Theo said.

Ashley overlapped him. "We need to work on that." They laughed, but judging by the look on Ashley's face, a nerve had been struck. "Usually, I take the backseat with our money and say, 'Oh, I trust you to handle it.' But then, when there's a problem, I wish he'd communicated better. So, I contradict myself. I know that must be confusing for him." She looked over at Theo. "I'm raising two busy kids, and I don't have the same time to analyze every financial detail. But I still want to know what's happening and be part of it. Theo is making money, and I'm in the background, spending it without knowing the whole picture. It feels wrong, but honestly, the way things are now, I would rather gouge my eyes out than talk finances with Theo."

Theo looked off into the trees with a hurt expression. "Ouch."

Mans said, "It's tough, no doubt. We've been on that rollercoaster, too. There is hope, though, and the fact that you're talking about it now will change your lives."

Theo said, "I don't know why, but lately, I feel less *decisive*. My opinions have gotten blurry, and I'm afraid to stick my neck out and say what I think. It's like I don't have the energy to take risks anymore, or I'm afraid to. The stakes feel so high. It's shitty because I never used to be afraid of risk. I used to *love* it."

Ashley looked at her husband with surprise. He was never this open with strangers. He rarely was even with her. It was the first time she'd heard him mention this fear. She'd always assumed he was happy with how life turned out. She reached over and took Theo's hand, and he smiled at her awkwardly. This was new territory for both of them.

Seeing your partner's perspective allows you to feel and offer the unit a deeper wealth of experience.

10

Fantasies Born

Fourth Contest—14 June 2019
Last day at Permission Peak Lodge

After the morning fire, the girls entered the lodge while Mans and Theo headed to the tractor shed. They were leaving soon, and Mans asked Theo to help him bring some firewood to the lodge, as Orson would be gone for the day. Theo jumped at the offer—he was surprised at how eager he was to help out. It was like the air up there had given him more energy and enthusiasm for doing the most basic tasks.

"Mans, can I ask a random question?" Theo asked with a hint of hesitation.

"I love random questions!" Mans joked. "Shoot."

"I can't get over this panic whenever I think about not working as much as possible. How can I slow down and also feel financially secure?"

Mans took his hat off as Theo caught up to him. It was warming up now that they were in the sunshine. "Theo, when I finally sold my aggregate business and took account of what I had, it made me realize that success has to do with finances, but that's not the whole picture. The picture is *way* bigger than that."

Mans swept his foot across the ground, creating a clean canvas in the dry soil. "A friend told me about this a long time ago, and it really helped me understand how to transition into a different mindset and lifestyle. He called it the 'glow zone'—like a tachometer or a visual way to see if your life is bouncing off the rev limiter."

Mans knelt and drew the two axes of a graph in the soil. He then put an *H* beside the vertical axis and *M / E* under the horizontal axis. He looked up and said, "H for happiness, M for Money, and E for Effort."

He kept talking as he dragged his finger in the soil. "As you start applying effort, your happiness goes up relatively quickly. Then, happiness growth slows as you achieve a certain level of success and a sense of contentment. Then you get your second wind as you pour more energy into money, expel more effort, and your happiness boosts. But then something happens. Your money and effort continue growing, but your happiness levels off, or worse, starts to tip downward as all that effort takes its toll." He paused, then drew a flat line, finishing it off with a downward slope.

Theo had a bad feeling in the pit of his stomach. He was thinking of a heart rate machine flat lining with a long, drawn-out *beeeeep*. It reminded him of the anxiety he'd been having lately and his doctor's warnings.

Mans pointed to a spot on the diagram. "*The glow zone* is right before this flat-line zone, where your money and efforts produce a growing level of happiness. The longer you live in the flat-line area, the more permanent and normal it seems, where you would not remember how the glow zone feels."

Theo took out his phone and took a picture of Mans's dirt diagram.

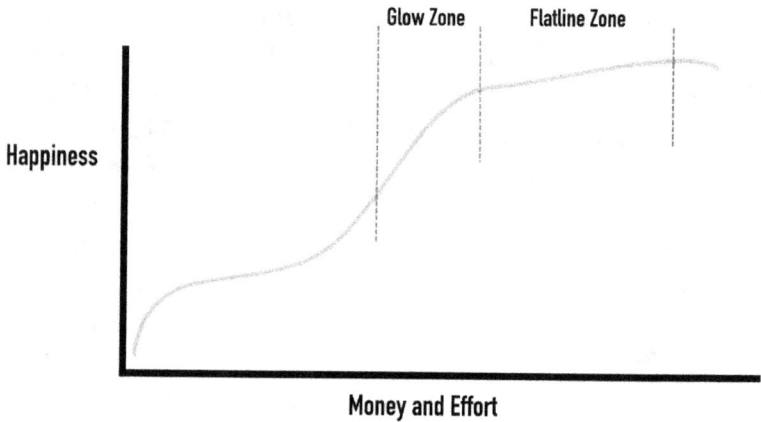

Glow Zone   Flatline Zone

Happiness

Money and Effort

Glow Zone: Where are you on the happiness/money/effort curve? If you have been adding new money to your pot and it requires more effort, yet you are not seeing an increase in happiness, it is time to focus on your mindset, not more money.

They reached the massive woodshed and began loading the tractor bucket with firewood. "I can see you're where I was a lot of years ago. You're at the point where you've reached that flat line and wonder why everything feels wrong. I don't want you to make the same mistake I did, which was to mindlessly keep going, thinking it would all work out in the end. The energy we spend in the front end of our lives deeply affects our energy at the back, and the distance between actions and consequences can be longer than you think."

The image of his dad sitting on the couch, griping about not wanting to golf anymore, flashed through Theo's mind. Where would he place his dad on this graph? How well did he know his dad, anyway?

As they rolled back toward the lodge with the wood, Theo realized he didn't want to leave. The lodge, he thought, represented a life cadence reset for him. He wondered how many other people could use a reset once every couple of years—to remove themselves from their lives, for a chance to recalibrate and recharge.

Ashley and Helena were in the foyer with the bags. They looked like they'd connected—they were laughing like old friends. "Chopper is fifteen minutes away," Helena said when they entered.

After the two couples exchanged hugs, Mans drove Theo and Ashley to the landing pad a few minutes before the helicopter arrived. Before they got out, Mans gave Theo a note with his and Helena's personal contact information. "Keep in touch, okay?"

As the rotor blades pounded the air and the chopper lifted, Theo gazed at the trees dropping away and felt a new exhilaration for something he couldn't put his finger on. He looked over at his wife, who took his hand and smiled.

Dodge the stalemate and let possibilities ignite when you start saying, "I'll do this as a short-term experiment."

11

Decision's Grip

Second Contest—3 July 2017
In the hills above Chilliwack, B.C.

The sound of a horn beeping made Theo look around as he grabbed his camera off the passenger seat and stepped out of the SUV. A Bobcat skid steer was coming around the corner of one of the modern-looking buildings. The entire complex had been conceptualized and recently built as a whole.

Theo had driven to meet a potential "Ultimate Picture of Wealth" subject: Kazuko Sato. The woman was a farmer from Japan who had built a small empire in the foothills east of Vancouver. Discovering her had come as a surprise; an old college buddy of his had told him about Kazuko while sharing his many failed attempts at a healthier diet. She was a snail farmer who had built up a 'boutique plantation' in southern B.C.

After researching Kazuko's work with snails and the incredible health benefits they seemed to offer, he was intrigued. She was clearly enjoying a successful business life. When he looked even closer and saw how much her customers were *paying* for her snails—and who some of her clients were—he emailed her and asked if he could drive out to meet her.

"You must be Theo," she said. "You can call me Kaz." She was older than he was expecting, for some reason, and not at all how he had pictured a farmer to be, even a snail farmer: small-framed, almost a foot shorter than Theo, with long, thick white hair pulled into a large bun on the top of her head. She wore light blue linen pants, an ancient pair of Converse shoes, and a dirt-smudged Rolling Stones T-shirt.

"Great to meet you!" Theo said. "I'm looking forward to learning about snails and hoping you can add a different perspective to the Ultimate Picture of Wealth contest. A booming snail business! That's pretty unusual."

Kaz laughed good-naturedly as she led the way to the closest building. She opened the door to the first greenhouse, and they entered a small holding room. "This first room is to regulate temperature. We heat the structure so we can have snails growing all year round. Please wipe your shoes here."

Theo did as he was told, and they moved into the main greenhouse.

The complex smelled surprisingly clean, although Theo didn't know what he thought it would smell like. The greenhouse was also tranquil. A young man working midway down a row raised his hand in greeting, then returned to work.

The snail beds were lined with blue plastic near the top, which Theo concluded was to keep the snails from escaping, as the plastic would be too slippery to move on. The whole thing had the feel of a clean, organized lab. There was nothing out of place.

Kaz went to a nearby shelf and picked up a pail of what looked like vegetable scraps. "What was the main motivation to start this operation?" Theo asked.

"I think I mentioned on the phone, but I broke my neck diving into a pool while on a vacation several years ago. It did not sever my spinal cord, thankfully, but my long recovery made me realize my life could have ended right there, not having accomplished anything. Middle management at an unnamed electronics company in Japan!" Kaz smiled at Theo. "I achieved so much for my employer but nothing for myself. My grandparents had lived in a small village, and as a girl, I was fascinated by watching how their little farm worked. I had treasured being close to the earth and missed it dearly. But I always thought there was no money in farming, and that type of labour was frowned upon, especially for women. So, I never pursued it."

She continued, "But after my accident, I decided to put my interests first for the first time in my life. I came to peace with the fact that changing my expectations didn't mean I was lowering them. I packed my things and moved from Japan to Canada." Kaz paused her story while she peeked under a section of the net. "I learned to see happiness in new things. I tried growing some different things, but I'm just experimenting. Snails are not a North American tradition, but in Japan, we enjoy snails all the time. It was comfort food. When I saw there were no organic snails grown in this area yet, I created my hutch and started selling them online and at food markets. I guess you could say it was a success."

Theo looked around at the vast greenhouse and the contently working employee making his way down the row. *A success? That's an understatement*, he thought.

Kaz continued. "We went from one small greenhouse and a small crop of snails we sold locally to shipping them worldwide. But it was important to me that we grew naturally and intentionally. We don't have massive production; it is still relatively small-scale. We take special care of each season of snails. We generate enough revenue to cover what we need. I employ twelve local people bouncing from job to job and getting nowhere, mostly immigrants and single women who couldn't make it work with the low wages offered to them elsewhere. Now, they are saving for their children's education and pursuing their dreams. We all work four days a week. Employees choose their days off, and we encourage taking time for an active lifestyle."

Theo estimated how many snails there must have been in that greenhouse and the two others like it. "Where do they all go, the snails? Are they all consumed as food?"

"No. Many companies buy them to use in anti-aging creams." She looked around at her greenhouse thoughtfully. "These creatures serve humans in so many ways. We treat them respectfully while they are under our care because our well-being is directly related to theirs." Kaz was very proud of her product and what she had built.

She's a genius, Theo thought.

When they walked into the packaging area to pick up Theo's online order, he said, "If you don't mind me asking, Kaz, it must have been a huge decision to leave everything behind and move to Canada. Wasn't that hard?"

She leaned her elbow on the counter and thought for a moment. "Well, Theo, my father always said that when you need to make a decision, go right to the worst-case scenario and decide if you can live with that. For me, the worst-case scenario if things didn't go well in Canada would have been to return to Japan and go back to a job like my old one. There was nothing to lose.

"The worst-case scenario of staying, though, would have been knowing I had never really attempted to live to my fullest potential and that I couldn't live with. When you make a decision, there are always many possible outcomes. Hanging around in those thoughts for too long is like decision quicksand. We must not get stuck on decisions. You will never do anything if you are scared of all that *could* happen. Can you imagine? I would have never had this beautiful farm."

She then handed him his box of frozen snails as he was visualizing decisions sinking in a bed of quicksand, and with that, they said goodbye.

He never ended up using Kaz as a subject, but he did take away a picture of his life if he slowed down long enough to consider what he really wanted and whether he could live with the worst-case scenario.

Before jumping in, ask yourself:
Can I live with the worst-case scenario?

12

Luck Altering Email

Fourth Contest—22 June 2019
Burnaby, B.C.

Theo lifted his finger from the mouse and sat back in his chair with a sigh. He stretched out his arms, cracked his neck, and thought about taking a break. He was tired of clicking through pictures. He and Ashley had been home from the lodge for a week, and today was the deadline to submit his entry for the contest. He knew that, win or not, this would be his last attempt.

Click—a picture of Roy and his fishing buddies. *Click*—more pictures of Roy. *Click, click.* Photos of the lodge and the lake. A picture of Mans and Helena, smiling. As crucial as this contest was to him, he was having trouble focusing. His mind kept returning to the lodge and what Mans and Helena had told them about their lives and what they'd learned. He leaned back on his creaking office chair with his hands behind his head and let his eyes drift to the shelf above his desk.

He reached out for the sizeable, intricate snail shell Kaz had given him as a souvenir, right there next to her picture. He picked it up and held it to his eyes for the millionth time. *Take a risk,* he could hear her tell him. What's the worst that could happen?

It was unmistakable that the overall flow in Theo's life had improved since returning from the lodge. He and Ashley had made love more often in the past week, and he was more patient with the kids than usual. He wasn't rushing off to work every morning. He had delegated more tasks to his project manager, Claire, and it had paid off: she'd proven herself and landed a couple of very lucrative contracts. Yes, something was shifting.

But, as he stared at the shell and its delicate lines curling into infinity, he realized that for a long time, he'd been waiting for a convincing enough reason to change his line of work. He felt trapped and bored. He was tired of doing what was expected of him.

His father's voice drifted through his head: "*When you get older, you don't feel like doing the things you used to.*" Those words gave him a chill. All that work, all that time spent saving and sacrificing, only to give up when it was his turn to enjoy? "What the hell," Theo said out loud.

Was there something out there for him and Ashley? Something different than what they'd imagined for themselves?

Just then, Ashley sauntered into his office with a cup of coffee, barefoot in an oversized T-shirt and shorts, munching on a piece of toast. "What are you working on?"

He turned to her, not yet ready to share what he was thinking. "I'm trying to decide what picture to submit to the contest."

She leaned over and looked at rows and rows of pictures, all of Roy, Bill, and John in various fishing poses. "When's the deadline?"

"Today."

"Oof," she said. "I'll leave you to it." She kissed him and patted his cheek affectionately, an old habit from their dating days that reappeared after they returned from the lodge. "Thank you for getting the girls' backpacks organized last night."

He sat there for a moment and started zoning out. Suddenly, he heard a notification ping. Absentmindedly, he clicked open his email and was surprised to see a message from the lodge's admin account. He clicked it open.

Hi Theo and Ashley,

I am writing to let you know some news. Mans had a stroke and has been taken to the hospital in Vancouver. He's stable now, but it looks like he and Helena will have to move to the city for the foreseeable future. They can no longer care for the lodge and are looking for management. They offered it to me, but I don't want the responsibility—I love it here, but I love my sanity more, lol. Their son isn't interested either. They thought that you two would be perfect for the job.

They aren't ready to talk yet, but Helena asked me to put this to you and tell you to think about it. And Mans had a special message for you: "Remember the fish in the pool." Whatever that means.

I think it's an incredible offer. I know you have your own business, Theo, but I could tell you were looking for something when you were up here. Maybe this is it?

Anyway, I got to get back at it. Think about it.

Orson

• • •

Theo put on his favourite Evel Knievel shirt, gave himself a pep talk, and went to find his wife. All morning, he'd been consumed with visions of himself leading fishing and biking trips through the mountains, Ashley and the kids coming up on weekends to enjoy all the benefits of the outdoors. It would be a whole new start and a new life for all of them. He'd pictured Ashley holding yoga workshops and the girls growing up close to nature.

When he was up at the lodge, an idea had come to him that seemed like a crazy fantasy. What if he created a retreat for those looking for clarity in their lives, for a chance to see the bigger picture? Now, amazingly, here was a chance to make that fantasy a reality, staring him right in the eye.

In a flash, he remembered something: his journal. He had recorded everything from the lodge, all those conversations, what he'd learned, and even everything he had not comprehended but had quickly jotted down for later. This was it. He wanted to use it and talk about it to anyone who would listen. He felt like he'd found his edge again.

Ashley had dropped the kids off at day camp and was working in the garden. It was a warm morning, and she had a large sun hat and shorts on, kneeling in the dirt. He walked over to her, put one hand on her shoulder, and started telling her about the email from Orson, leaving the part about managing the lodge out. He wasn't *quite* sure how she would react.

She put down her tool and stood up, brushing soil off her knees. "Poor Helena," she said. "Should we go visit them?"

"Ah, yeah, I suppose we should."

She put her hands on her hips and thought. "Who's going to take care of the lodge? Orson, I guess? Too bad we can't do it," she laughed. "I would love to go back up there."

Theo took a deep breath. He couldn't have asked for a better moment. He reached out and took her hands in his. "Well, actually, I didn't tell you all of it. They did offer management to Orson, but he isn't interested, and their son doesn't want it either. So, apparently, the job's ours, if *we* want it," Theo paused, letting it sink in for a moment, "and I think we should think about it. It will mean taking a pay cut, but think about the lifestyle! Think about the girls being up there, in that serene nature, how healthy it would be for them. I think we can still do well. Maybe we can even talk to Mans about a succession plan. We're still young, we enjoy challenges, we love each other, and, well, I want to do it."

Her eyes widened, and there was a tense moment. He could see her fighting with herself—she wore the look she always had whenever he suggested he would like to buy an expensive, high-powered, single-seat toy. He could almost hear what was coming: *Are you kidding me?* He felt his hackles rise. *Why do I even bother*, he wondered. But then he remembered how they'd been reconnecting and decided to keep quiet and let her think.

She shook her head and looked down for a minute, thinking. Then, she seemed to come to a decision. To his relief, her face softened. She looked him in the eye and said, "I've always kind of wished I could home-school the girls. This could be our chance."

Theo felt the sun brighten.

"But promise me one thing," Ashley continued. "If we *do* this, we go all-in. I saw how happy you were at that lodge. I want that guy to be around more often. As long as the numbers make sense, let's look into it. Carefully. Properly. And we make the decision *together*."

Theo gave Ashley a long, tight hug and said, "We won't half-ass it, I promise." He gave her a hard, excited kiss. She giggled and pushed him off.

"I know what you're doing for the rest of the day," she said. "I want a full report later. And don't forget about the contest." She winked, picked up her rake, and returned to the garden bed.

Theo was feeling light and hopeful. He was so happy. It wasn't a done deal yet, but the way he felt right now was all he needed to know he was on the right path. He was finally returning the reins from a force he hadn't known existed.

He went back inside, practically floating towards his office when suddenly he was gripped with fear. His chest constricted. *What the hell am I thinking?* He imagined his dad's reaction when he told him that he and Ashley were moving their entire life to a remote fishing lodge up in the mountains. He would think Theo was insane. And he would be right.

"Shit." He stared at his computer screen, panicking, his heart racing and his eyes wandering over the set of photos that he'd been scanning through earlier. One caught his eyes, and he leaned closer, suddenly remembering a conversation he'd had with Mans on his first day at the lodge about protection:

Protect your back and focus on what's in front of you.

13

Cold Plunge Blindness

Fourth Contest—11 June 2019
Back at the Lodge

Theo locked his camera gear into the watertight rear compartment for the trip back to the lodge.

"Make sure both latches and the overlap strap are secure on that thing," Mans said. He turned the machine around and worked it out of the lake zone, taking a different trail. After a minute, he stopped, locked in the differential, and pointed the machine straight at an impossible-looking rocky rise. Then, he slowly crawled the machine up a section that Theo thought would have been difficult, even on foot. But the tires held, and as they crested the hill, all they could see was the hood of the machine and the sky. Theo's heart jumped.

Then, the ground leveled out and there in front of them was a meadow that darkened into a wetland at the far end, sparkling with water and bristling with bunch grasses and low-lying shrubs. A rushing creek blocked their way to the meadow dotted with wildflowers. The top ridge of the Rocky Mountains rose far in the background.

Mans eased the UTV back down the bluff into the meadow. They were about to cross the creek, which looked to Theo to be far too deep to cross in the machine, but there were tracks on both sides, so this was something that happened regularly. He saw Mans check the differential and four-wheel-drive again, and before he knew what was happening, Mans once again floored the machine—straight into the middle of the creek. In an instant, the ice-cold water rushed over the hood, hitting Theo smack in the chest and enveloping his body up to his armpits. He had a moment of panic when he thought he was going under, but then, in a flash, they launched out the other side, water pouring off of them and the UTV.

"I call that the *cleanse crossing*," Mans laughed, stopping.

Theo spat, "I call you an asshole! You're lucky—what if my camera wasn't locked up?"

Mans kept laughing and slapped Theo's shoulder amiably. "It is, though!"

Theo was still spluttering. He jumped out and was trying to wring out his soaking clothes, furious about what could have happened to his camera, not to mention having soaking wet clothes for the rest of the ride back. He noticed that Mans' hiking khakis and shirt were both quick-dry. *Of course. The balls on this guy!* Mans was right, though: his camera was fine. And he had to admit, the shock of icy water had left his skin buzzing and invigorated. He felt great. He was about to turn and say as much when he noticed Mans staring at something far away.

Following his gaze, Theo saw a moose cow and a calf had emerged from the trees at the meadow's far end. The mama was on high alert and watching them. The whole meadow seemed to be frozen in time.

"Why isn't she taking off?" Theo asked in a low voice.

"She knows me," Mans said quietly. "This cow used to raise calves here a few years ago, but I haven't seen her for a while. I recognize her because her legs are a bit lighter-coloured than normal. It's perfect for them here. They are sheltered from the harsh weather and have lots of vegetation. A young wolf started hanging around here a couple of years ago, then two wolves, and then three. She left for higher ground, which was safer, but there wasn't great vegetation. I found her last year, over on the other side of the lodge, where there's a rocky bluff. She was very skinny, and she wasn't moving around. I guess she didn't want to risk coming to the meadow."

"So why is she here now?" Theo asked.

"Well, I think I know," Mans said, taking out a pair of binoculars and peering toward the moose. "See, I hated seeing her suffering like that, so last year, I took the matter into my own hands. I spent some money on what I thought could be a solution. I built that enclosure about a dozen feet high and twice as long down there. Orson helped. It's V-shaped, and we built the natural fences out of small tree logs set two inches apart, so you can still see through it."

Theo looked where Mans was pointing, shielding his eyes from the bright mid-day sun. Sure enough, there was a structure at the meadow's far end that he hadn't noticed because it blended in with the other trees. "Looks like a blind," he said, moving slowly to get his camera out.

Mans explained how his idea would provide the moose a way to enjoy the food and water of the meadow with the added security of the wall on two sides.

"She could feed while still being able to watch for danger," he said. "And if the wolves did come to call, she would only have to defend half her position instead of being completely exposed from all sides." Mans placed his hands on his hips and smiled. "I wasn't sure if it would work. But here she is, and with a calf, too. Let's see if we can get a bit closer without spooking her. Just what we need is to scare her off again."

They returned to the UTV and crept slowly around the meadow's perimeter, as far from the moose and her calf as they could get. She watched but seemed calm. Mans cut the engine before they got too close. Theo raised his camera and took a few photos of the cow and her calf, with the tall protective blind rising behind them.

"How did you get the idea to build that blind?" Theo asked as they were heading back.

Mans watched the trail ahead as they wound their way through the trees. "I guess I got it from thinking about my situation: protecting my back and focusing on what's in front of me," he replied.

Theo looked at him. "What do you mean?"

But before he knew what was happening, Mans was shouting, "Hang on!" and Theo went for his second cold dip in the creek.

*Secure your position first, assess your surroundings,
and then get strategic and review opportunities.*

14

Graphic Adventures

Fourth Contest—22 June 2019
At Home

Theo picked up his notepad and turned to a blank page. At the top, he wrote: *Manage the lodge.*

It's a great to-do item. Now what? He stared at the pictures on the shelf again. Then he clicked on his photos on the monitor and found the one he was looking for: Mans' drawing in the dirt on the side of the path—the glow zone. Things started clicking into place.

Balance. Lifestyle. Values.

Risk. Protection. Edge.

In the centre of the row of framed photos above his head was a picture of himself shaking Omar Ansari's hand just after the man's big meeting in Austin. There was a goofy grin on Theo's face as he thanked the man who had told him about his wealth edge. He stared at it, thinking, and then, in a flash of clarity, he saw it all working together. He saw the *plan*.

Feeling like a mad scientist, Theo scribbled notes for thirty minutes. He paused only once. A smooth, white stone he'd picked up at the lodge was on his desk—he rolled it around in his palm, thinking about the fish that had risked it all and reaped the rewards.

He noted all their financial facets, like insurance amounts and investment accounts. What was the worst-case scenario? He or Ashley could die suddenly. He could get sick or injured or have a mental breakdown from the stress. They could get divorced. *I'm getting into the weeds here*, he thought.

He noted on his to-do list: "Talk to Ashley about counselling and buy a book on successful relationships."

He took a deep breath, brought out his notes, and planned to share them with Ashley.

He could see she was trying to follow what he was saying, but she had a pained, confused expression. Eventually, she said, "Theo, I'm just not one hundred percent getting it. There are too many moving parts. I understand that we will shift our lifestyle and spending habits and less profit from the business. But all the financial elements are overwhelming me right now. I need to see it visually. That's just the way my brain works. Can you draw me a simple picture?"

Theo felt a rush of annoyance. Why couldn't she see it? But he also remembered that he needed to communicate better with Ashley. She had just communicated what she needed, which was a chance for him to communicate back. He stood up and said, "Yes, I'll be right back."

Theo went to his computer and pulled up the photo he'd snapped of the wealth plan he and Carlos had drawn based on scuba dive planning. Then he rummaged in his desk and pulled out the limp bar napkin on which Chloë Ellis had coached him to include a focus on relationships, self, and mental health in his plan.

He sipped his now-cold coffee and reread his notes, then started drawing. Using Chloë and Carlos' drawings as a template, he sketched out all the important aspects of their lives, including their relationships, health, and spending.

He needed to step away from his business and let it run itself. He needed to automate as much as he could. He would not disappear, but he needed to start transitioning the business onto his key employees and put the brakes on the drive for limitless growth. A succession plan at his age seemed odd, but he had a goal now, a more significant calling than making money. He looked up at the snail shell. He also wanted to change people's lives positively.

He sat back down on the couch and touched Ashley's arm. "Okay. Can we take a few minutes to look at this? I can explain it better now." He showed her the diagram. "This is something we can check in on from time to time to clarify our goals and to help us communicate better about anything, like what we each want from ourselves and each other. It's the whole picture."

Ashley looked at him and smiled, setting her phone down. In all their years of marriage, she had never heard the words *communicate better* from Theo or gotten the feeling that he thought about what goals they had *together*. She repositioned herself to face him. It felt wonderful to see Theo making communicating with her a priority. "Yes, please. I'm intrigued."

Theo began. "We now have a common goal: to put the business in the background and manage the lodge. And I want more. I also want to *use* the lodge to teach others what I've been learning about wealth. Any thoughts so far?"

Ashley was nodding along as he spoke. Theo could see her wheels turning—she was getting on board. "Yeah, and Mans and Helena played a big part in that. I felt so *clear* up there like we had space to get perspective. I see what you mean about sharing it with others."

He then pointed to what he had drawn. "This is the whole big picture. It has a personal priority pyramid and a road map that brings to light all the facets of getting us where we want to be." Theo was proud of his depiction of everything happening in his head, and Ashley seemed impressed.

Now, she could visualize all the disorderly thoughts coming together beautifully into order, into a whole new perspective—a whole new life.

Theo felt a massive relief watching her pore over their finances, like a weight had been lifted off his shoulders. The fun part would be figuring out how to make it work and start their life's new chapter. Theo looked forward to seeing what the universe had in store for him in the coming months. He was ready for anything.

Behind them, the clock on the kitchen wall ticked past one, passing the deadline for the "Ultimate Picture of Wealth" contest. Theo pulled his wife close and clicked the TV to life. She left her phone on the table.

When you create and communicate a clear plan, "I'm in" will be part of your partner's vocabulary.

Don't Mind If I Do

Theo sat down across from his dad and took a deep breath. He'd invited him to the lodge under the pretence of a father-son bonding trip, a gift for the man's seventieth birthday. This was their last day there, after three days of enjoying the fresh air, good food, and epic fishing with Orson as their guide.

They enjoyed each other's company again after a long time. Evenings were spent next to a fire down by the lake, drinking beer and talking, laughing over stories, and sharing details about their lives. Theo finally connected with his dad in a way he had never been.

He hadn't told his dad he and Ashley were taking over management of the lodge yet and had wanted to let him experience the magic of the place before breaking the news.

They were in a great place of openness, and his dad was as relaxed as he probably would ever be, yet Theo still wasn't sure how his dad would react once he shared the news.

"Well, Dad, what do you think of this place?" He asked, cracking a beer and handing it over. They were seated in the lodge's living room in front of the crackling fire. It was late in the season, and there were only two other guests—a couple who had gone out on a long hike and weren't due back until later that day. They were about to enjoy some appetizers that

Orson was preparing—the comforting sounds and smells of cooking wafted from the kitchen.

Ted grinned and leaned over to clink bottles with his son. "I love it," he said. "This place is special, just like you said. I get why you wanted to come back up here. I'm glad you brought me son. Thank you."

"Would you like to spend more time here?" Theo's nervousness had passed, and he was excited to tell his dad the news.

His dad raised an eyebrow. "Why?"

"Well, because this lodge is about to become a big part of our lives—Ashley's, mine, and the girls. And I hope you and Mom's as well." Theo paused to let it sink in for a moment. "The owner, Mans Jonsson, had a stroke and can't run the place anymore. He asked me and Ashley to take it over. And, well, we said yes. I'll be coming up here on the weekends over the winter to help Orson transition, and Ash and the girls will move up with me full-time in the spring. I know you'll say it's impulsive—" Theo rushed on before his dad could interrupt "—but we have it all worked out, and it makes sense. We're excited about it." Theo felt like a teenager, trying to convince his dad to get on board with something crazy that he wanted.

Ted was quiet, like Ashley when he'd first broached the idea to her. Theo watched as the wheels turned in his dad's head. Finally, he looked up.

"You know, Theo," he said. "When you told me that you entered that contest again, and I got so mad about it, it wasn't because I thought your business needed that much attention. It was because I could see that the contest was a distraction for you from what you needed to figure out in your life. I didn't know how to tell you, so I made it about the business.

"But really, I didn't think that a photography contest was where you should be putting your energy. You seemed lost, like you were using it to escape your problems. Instead of dealing with your issues with Ashley and your money, you were running off to pursue something I knew you weren't passionate about."

Theo looked at his dad, amazed. He had no idea his dad thought this much about him. Last of all, in such an insightful way. "You didn't think I was passionate about the contest?"

His dad looked him straight in the eye. "Theo, I have never seen you as happy and rejuvenated as you were when you were going off on all your adventures when you were younger. You dismissed those days as your frivolous college years before you became serious about a business career. But I saw that as your calling. You were so good at guiding, and being outside brought out the best in you. From where I stood, that was your passion, but you left it behind when you got into marketing. So, when I saw you running after these side projects, searching for adventure, I got frustrated because I felt like I knew what you were missing. You were missing that spark, that *edge* you had when you were younger."

Theo couldn't believe his dad had just mentioned his "edge." He threw his head back and laughed out loud. "Are you kidding me?" He got up, went over to his dad, and hugged him awkwardly. "You have no idea how good it is to hear you say that," he said, tapping his bemused father's shoulder.

"Well, I'm glad to say it, son."

"Why didn't you tell me before?" Theo was stunned that all these years, his dad had been thinking the same thing he was: he'd been missing a spark he used to have.

His dad shrugged. "What could I have possibly said? 'Son, you're in the wrong career'? Yeah, right! It was something you had to discover for yourself. Anyway, this contest helped you find it. I guess it was good for something after all."

Theo thought of all the pictures of Roy and his friends that he'd taken that summer, all gone to waste because he'd missed the deadline. He shook his head. Suddenly, it stopped seeming so important when he discovered he wanted to live at the lodge. "I think this place will be good for us, Dad. Very, very good, for all of us."

Ted replied, "It already has been, son." Theo could feel the content in his dad's tone.

Orson appeared at that moment with a massive tray of steaming hors d'oeuvres. "Gentlemen?" He said, while setting the food on the low table between them. "May I interest you in some scotch?"

"Don't mind if I do, good buddy," Theo said, glowing with a joy that he hoped was only the beginning of a brand-new state of mind. "Don't mind if I do."

Chapter Takeaways

My Story

You need more "ands" in your life.

Behind Grandma Mae's Microwave

Don't pass away with the ghosts of your dreams behind the microwave.

The Question

Ask yourself: Is the mission I am on worthy to me?

Chapter 1: Think Fast, She's Hot

Start enjoying what you desire for dinner and stop gazing down the right side of the menu.

Chloe's Takeaway: Are you saving too much for too long?

Chapter 2: Danger Zone Thinking

But, more often than not, exciting adventures are not born from an endless series of logical thinking.

Ted's Takeaway: Are you living too conservatively for the stage of life you are in?

Chapter 3: High Altitude Awakening

When was the last time you ventured into uncharted territory? Is it finally time to create a few new stories in your life?"

André's takeaway: Stay creative and interesting to yourself.

Chapter 4: Grab Another Gear

Your Unique Ability is a superpower more capable than all investment and career choices.

Omar's Takeaway: Let amateurs walk behind other people's whim while you run with your talent.

Chapter 5: Risk Reward

People are programmed to follow the herd, but to have a world of abundance, we must embrace the possibilities of the unknown outcome.

Mans' Takeaway: Learning we have another dimension of achievement is easier to find with classmates who already think like we want to.

Chapter 6: Is Enough Worth It

If no one was watching or caring about your increased success, would you keep grinding for a little longer?

Mans' Takeaway: Tame your stress by pruning your life commitments, lowering your expectations, and watching the recurring quality time flow into your life.

Chapter 7: Magic Apology

Your trajectory to wealth will instantly change with a heartfelt "sorry," even though you may not think you have to say it.

Theo's Takeaway: A "brainstorming meeting" with your partner is a safe place—no judgement, no one is allowed to get mad, and nothing is set in stone.

Chapter 8: Diving Fearlessly

With life priorities clarified, the daredevil of your identity can rise from the ashes.

Carlo's Takeaway: Deliberately jeopardizing your future may seem reckless to old beliefs.

Chapter 9: Chaotic Automation

Seeing your partner's perspective allows you to feel and offer the unit a deeper wealth of experience.

Helena's Takeaway: Automating your numbers turns one week in Mexico to one month in Maui.

Chapter 10: Fantasies Born

Dodge the stalemate and let possibilities ignite when you start saying, "I'll do this as a short-term experiment."

Mans' Takeaway: Happiness is not born from the marriage of money and effort.

Chapter 11: Decision's Grip

Before jumping in, ask yourself: Can I live with the worst-case scenario?

Kaz's Takeaway: Fixating on low-probability events limits potential.

Chapter 12: Luck Altering Email

Protect your back and focus on what's in front of you.

Theo's Takeaway: Luck will find you in groups of other achieving people.

Chapter 13: Cold Plunge Blindness

Secure your position first, assess your surroundings, and then get strategic and review opportunities.

Mans' Takeaway: As your life evolves, are your ideas evolving?

Chapter 14: Graphic Adventures

When you create and communicate a clear plan, "I'm in" will be part of your partner's vocabulary.

Ashley's Takeaway: The feeling of certainty doesn't come in as an email saying, "You are approved to now take Fridays off."

Resources and Further Reading

Books

Achor, Shawn. *The Happiness Project: How a Positive Brain Fuels Success in Work and Life*. Crown, 2018.

Clason, George S. *Richest Man in Babylon: The Success Secrets of the Ancients*. Penguin, 2002.

Cook, Steve. *Lifeonaire: An Uncommon Approach to Wealth, Success, and Prosperity*. Lifeonaire Promotions, 2018.

Deans, Thomas William. *Every Family's Business: 12 Common Sense Questions to Protect Your Wealth*. Détente Financial Press, 2009.

Ferriss, Timothy. The 4-Hour Work Week: Escape 9–5, Live Anywhere, and Join the New Rich. Harmony/Rodale, expanded & updated 2009.

García, Héctor, and Francesc Miralles. *Ikigai: The Japanese Secret to a Long and Happy Life*. Penguin, 2017.

Gerber, Michael. E. *The E-Myth Revisited: Why Most Small Businesses Don't Work and What to Do About It*. HarperCollins, 2004.

Harris, Russ. *The Happiness Trap: How to Stop Struggling and Start Living*. Shambhala, 2008.

Hill, Napoleon. *Think and Grow Rich: This Book Could Be Worth a Million Dollars to You*. Random House, 1987.

Pasricha, Neil. *Happiness Equation: Want Nothing + Do Anything = Have Everything*. Penguin, 2016.

Pasricha, Neil. *You Are Awesome: How to Navigate Change, Wrestle with Failure, and Live an Intentional Life*. Simon & Schuster, 2020.

Sharma, Robin. *The 5 AM Club: Own Your Morning. Elevate Your Life*. HarperCollins, 2018.

Ware, Bronnie. *The Top Five Regrets of the Dying. A Life Transformed by the Dearly Departing*. Hay House, 2019.

Articles, Blogs, Podcasts and Websites

Ferriss, Tim. *The Tim Ferris Show* podcast. https://tim.blog/podcast/

Kwick, Jim. https://jimkwik.com/

McKay, Brett & Kate. The Art of Manliness podcast. https://www.artofmanliness.com/podcast/

Mineo, Liz Mineo. "Harvard study, almost 80 years old, has proved that embracing community helps us live longer, and be happier," The Harvard Gazette, April 11, 2017. https://news.harvard.edu/gazette/story/2017/04/over-nearly-80-years-harvard-study-has-been-showing-how-to-live-a-healthy-and-happy-life/

Pasricha, Neil. *1000 Awesome Things* blog. http://1000awesomethings.com/

Rogan, Joe. *The Joe Rogan Experience* podcast. https://www.joerogan.com/

Shetty, Jay. *Jay Shetty Podcast.* https://jayshetty.me/podcast/

About Dustin Serviss

Dustin Serviss attended the University of British Columbia on a sports scholarship, where he received a diploma. Upon graduation, he explored a civil engineering career and quickly pivoted to the financial services industry, spending eight prosperous and valuable years working as a senior associate with an advisory group before launching Serviss Wealth Management Inc. in 2014.

Dustin holds the Certified Financial Planner, Chartered Life Underwriter, Chartered Investment Manager, and Certified Health Specialist designations. He is a lifelong learner, especially in the area of wealth research and planning and has personal experience in investing (real estate, stock, and crypto) and complex insurance strategies for business owners for nearly two decades. He strives to challenge his beliefs, let in new ideas, and broaden his horizons. His dynamic learning habits have led him to where he is today, expanding his pool of knowledge and eagerly sharing it with his clients and friends.

Never one to shy away from a hard pivot or a new opportunity, Dustin has learned through experience the value of gut decisions and taking the road less travelled. He leverages this knowledge into a practice dedicated to the wealth and lifestyle design space, helping potential entrepreneurs get clear on how to spend more yet remain financially responsible. If anyone can be said to be "walking his walk," it's Dustin.

Dustin has a knack for turning complex concepts into easy-to-digest ideas and sharing them through his writing, online courses, and podcast appearances. He also hosts his own podcast, *The Picture of Wealth*. He has spoken for various crowds across Canada, sharing his vision.

When not working or speaking, Dustin and his wife and two sons enjoy an active and adventurous Okanagan lifestyle, participate in various outdoor and cultural activities, and appreciate the people, fantastic food and wine, and vibrant West Coast culture.

If you are looking for a professional speaker for your event or require bulk book orders of this book for your organization, please contact info@servisswealth.com

www.ingramcontent.com/pod-product-compliance
Lightning Source LLC
Chambersburg PA
CBHW071433210326
41597CB00020B/3775